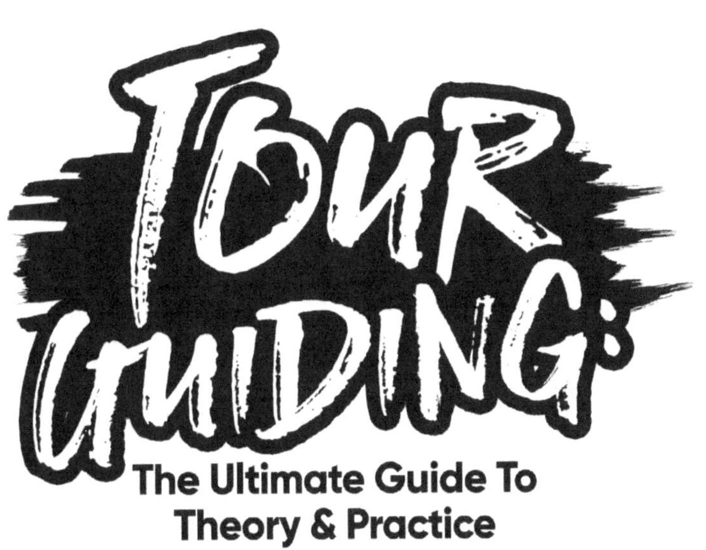

TOUR GUIDING:

The Ultimate Guide To Theory & Practice

COSMOS SRACOOH • KWAKU PASSAH SNR

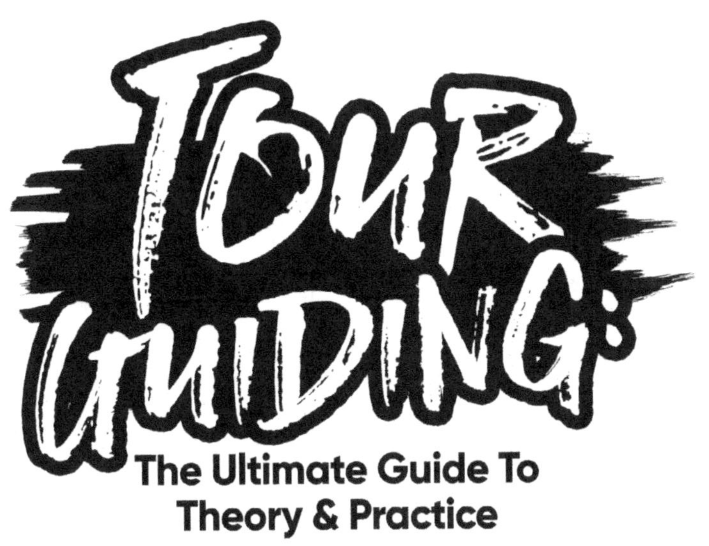

COSMOS SRACOOH • KWAKU PASSAH SNR

TOUR GUIDING: THE ULTIMATE GUIDE TO THEORY AND PRACTICE

ISBN: 97899889023 6 0

Editorial Team

Kofi Akpabli

Nana Awere Damoah

Cover Design and Book Layout by

Nene Buer Boyetey

P O Box NM 78, Nima, Accra, Ghana

Email: bigglesmultimedia@gmail.com

Tel: +233 244 634 204

Published by

DAkpabli & Associates

P O Box 7465, Accra North, Accra, Ghana

Tel: +233 264 339 066 | +233 244 704 250 | +233 247 896 375

Email: info@dakpabli.com

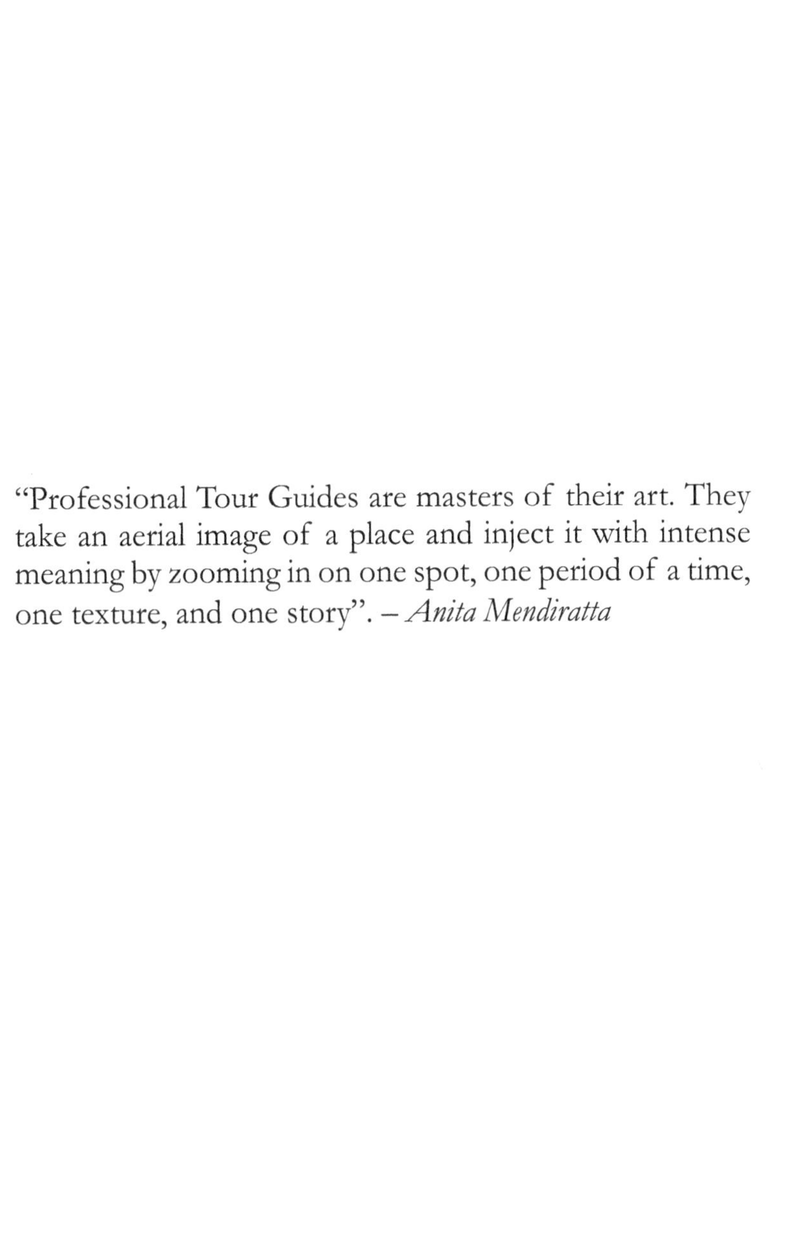

"Professional Tour Guides are masters of their art. They take an aerial image of a place and inject it with intense meaning by zooming in on one spot, one period of a time, one texture, and one story". – *Anita Mendiratta*

TABLE OF CONTENTS

FROM THE AUTHORS

The idea and ultimate decision to write this book stem from a concern, a passion to see tourists have the full benefit of tourism experience. Oftentimes, tourists look up to the Tour Guide for the full enjoyment of the tour. The tour guide, of course, is seen as the expert who is to be trusted by the guest. Hence, the tour guide must be appropriately resourced and well prepared in order to not disappoint or "lead his guests astray".

In a number of instances, however, many have assumed that anyone can play the role of a tour guide. The professional element has therefore, sadly, been negated. This state of affairs has led to a dilution of the quality of guiding that is offered at many destinations.

This book comes out as an antidote to the anomaly. First, it comes as a professional tool in tour guiding training and practice. Secondly, it becomes a readily available and accessible material for all who have genuine interest to enter the business of tour guiding. The motivations are enriched by over two decades of experience as trainers and practitioners in tour guiding. Interactions and engagements with our trainees, colleague guides, industry players, and tourists, over the years, serve as a great impetus to this project, and for which we salute them all.

Two particular persons who have been of invaluable assistance with their rich information, time and know-how deserve our acknowledgement here. Mr. Nkunu Akyea and Mr. Sammy Ashford Banibensu (Uncle Sam), we owe you both. And to Mr. Apollinaire Panou (Almighty Apollo), accept our profound appreciation for your persistent encouragement.

We hope this book will be a modest contributor to the shaping
of Tour Guiding in the broad spectrum of tourism promotion.

Cosmos Sracooh   *Kwaku Passah Snr*

PREFACE

My wanderlust has always inspired me to not set my eyes solely overseas but to enjoy my country and its backyard of sweet-scented roses and unique diversity. I have gained much experience and learnt many things from all the travels I have made over the years through prior research, exploration and from tour guides.

The role of the tour guide cannot be underestimated. It is a lot of work, responsibility and exchange to get to expand your mind and spirit, which is priceless. Tour guide training is essential to acquire the knowhow and the confidence in delivering quality services.

I met the authors of this book in the early-mid 90s when I ventured into the tourism industry as a tour operator. Our interactions were very positive and we quickly realised how beneficial our relationship could be developed further to complement our businesses. We shared information and views and have continued to do same to date. The unquestionable quality of guides produced under their direction was always the preferred guides for hire by our company.

Kwaku Passah Snr. and I were fortunate to become initial members of the Tour Operators Union of Ghana in 2000 and to serve as executives, where some of our ideas played a major role in the association in the area of Domestic Tourism Awareness creation.

The quest for tour guiding excellence – and a passion to give tourists an experiential benefit – has been a driving force for the authors. They have both spent years as trusted tour guides and have imparted their knowledge to many, lecturing and organising workshops throughout the country.

"The tour guide must be appropriately resourced and well-prepared in order to not disappoint or lead the guests astray."

This statement sums up the all-encompassing intent of this *Tour Guiding Book*. The practising tour guide should explore and seek for added knowledge and techniques to enhance their performance in this dynamic tourism industry. The scope of coverage is vast and will be very useful as a general guide book for any reader seeking access to the history, geography and our rich cultural heritage.

The best holidays are always timeouts from the usual daily routine. In this regard, Ghana with its numerous magical and diverse culture, flora and fauna lives up to its promise as well as expectations. The fact is that you can take a step back in time to do the pre-colonial/colonial with its slave trade era to post-independence and the changing epochs in Ghana. Who will tell the story and how will it be told? This will be done effectively by the one who has read and understood the written works of Kwaku Passah Snr. and Cosmos Sracooh, who have shared their expertise and experience as masters of the game.

I believe this *Tour Guiding Book* will be a great resource filling the gap for travellers and students alike. It will enhance, enlighten and give the reader confidence in rendering good service as well as knowledge to communicate clearly and responsibly on destination Ghana.

Mrs. Stella W. Appenteng,
CEO Apstar Tours Limited,
Accra, Ghana

FOREWORD

Tour Guiding: The Ultimate Guide to Theory and Practice is a handy, practical and contextually relevant book that simplifies our understanding of the tourism landscape in Ghana. Tourism is key to a nation's development. Hence, successive governments have promoted tourism through initiatives such as PANAFEST (Pan African Historical Theater Festival) and the *Year of Return* which attracted many foreign tourists to Ghana recently.

Passah and Sracooh's book contributes immensely to the literature on the tourism industry in Ghana. Informed by their long engagement with the tourism industry in Ghana through training and hosting of tourists, the authors provide an experience-based comprehensive exposition on Ghana's Tourism Sector within the context of history, politics, socio-culture and the economy.

The book has been structured into two key parts. Part One introduces the reader to the basic components of tourism. It explains the concept of a tour guide and describes the qualities required of a tour guide. The reader is further taken through the various types of tourism, the nitty-gritty of tourism and terminologies associated with the industry.

Part Two focuses on the contextual realities of Ghana's tourism landscape by describing in detail the geographical, political, historical and traditional profiles of the country. Key traditional institutions, and rituals such as rites of passage, chieftaincy institution, traditional festivals and artifacts like kente and stool which reflect both Ghanaian material and immaterial cultures are highlighted.

The most intriguing part of the book relates to the exposition on the naming system of the Akans. The naming, which is based on the days of the week, tends to be of great fascination to many foreigners and tourists.

The authors are credited with the linkage they establish between tourism and the Sustainable Development Goals (SDGs). This is an innovation that should be of great interest to tourists across the globe. What I admire most about the book relates to the lucid language, simplistic presentation style, detailed table of contents and comprehensiveness of the information provided. I recommend the book not only to industry players but also educationists (lecturers/teachers) and learners (students) at the various levels of our educational system, and in diverse fields outside tourism.

It is a book that should be read by all prospective tourists and readers interested in understanding the historical, socio-cultural, and economic contexts of Ghana's tourism industry. It may also be of relevance to policy makers.

As a Sociologist, I find the contents very relevant to the socio-cultural dimensions of tourism in our country. Students of sociology will also benefit from this book. The book is highly recommended to anyone who desires to gain an in-depth knowledge and understanding about Ghanaian culture and the nation's tourism landscape.

Ayekoo!!! Messrs Passah and Sracooh for availing your knowledge to both local and international audience.

Dr. Georgina Yaa Oduro,

Senior Lecturer, Department of Sociology and Anthropology, Director – Centre for Gender Research, Advocacy and Documentation (CEGRAD), University of Cape Coast, Ghana

INTRODUCTION

Tour Guiding remains a critical activity in providing the guiding experience for the tourist. The professional Tour Guide, who acts as the link between the tourist and the realisation of the latter's dreams, is an important player in shaping the tourism experience of the visitor.

This book has two-fold objectives. First, it is aimed at improving and enhancing – through proper industry orientation and techniques – the performance of tour guides. Secondly, it is to give adequate practical guidance to all students of tourism, particularly students offering Tourism at the Technical Universities and other tertiary institutions. The book is targeted to make them more efficient, productive and competitive so as to increase their marketability and productivity, as well as raise the product value of the destination concerned.

In the light of these objectives, the book is in two parts. **Part One** is composed of general guiding techniques and elements that are required for comprehensive delivery to result in that positive guiding experience sought by the guest. **Part Two** comprises some specific information and titbits on Ghana as is relevant to guiding within Ghana.

The unique aspect of this book is that the style is quite distinct in its objective as a self-training tool. Hence, there is a departure from the status-quo in terms of sentence structure. Much of the material is presented in bullet points and therefore not necessarily in complete sentences. This is deliberate as it is judged, in this context, to be the most effective method to ensure effectiveness.

PART ONE

GENERAL GUIDING TECHNIQUES

EFFECTIVE TOUR GUIDING

Tour guiding is a very comprehensive task that entails almost all aspects of human life. It therefore requires for the practitioner, a thorough and adequate preparation that captures all areas of interest in order to be effective and efficient. To this end, training for this onerous but interesting profession must not take anything for granted. Sadly however, one comes across tour guides who sometimes mess themselves up simply because they may have downplayed the importance of issues such as personal and environmental hygiene, among others.

To have a full grasp of the areas of importance, and to be fully ready, the business of tour guiding has been looked at, in this book, under the following aspects.

- Physiological – appreciation of the guide's physical qualities

- Environmental – both working environment and ecological resources

- Social – friendly and accommodating

- Educative – information and gained understanding of destination thanks to the guide's presence and facilitation

- Safety and comfort – guest's life not jeopardized due to negligence, over-anxiety and/or incompetence

- Psychological – self-esteem, happy to associate with such a guide

- Economic – value for money paid for guide's services

Who is a tour guide?

A tour guide is a qualified and licensed person who:

- Meets, welcomes, accompanies, and conducts guests (visitors) around specific sites/attractions/facility in specific locations or areas (e. g. Tafi monkey sanctuary and cultural village), a region or the country as a whole, and

- Provides well-researched, special and relevant information, explanations and interpretations about the sites, cultural practices and sometimes on thematic subjects. Information, explanations, interpretations, etc., have to do with varied areas of interest e.g. history, ecology, landscape and natural beauty, culture, heritage, socio-economic life, slavery/slave trade, etc. while…

- Ensuring the comfort, safety and well-being of guests

As a tour guide, you are the conveyor-belt or bridge between the tourist and the destination community. The tour guide is also the link between the tourist and the realization of his dreams. The tour guide is a 'civilian diplomat' who breathes life into the hidden stories behind the treasures, making history come alive. The treasures include the environment, ecology, people, culture, etc.

In this context, it is necessary to have an appropriate functional definition of tourism namely **"the celebration, showcasing and sharing of ecology, culture and identity"**.

Specific duties and responsibilities of the tour guide

By way of summary, these are the main duties and responsibilities of the Tour guide:

- Meeting and welcoming guests at the point of arrival
- Explaining to guests the fee structure and their benefits to the community
- Explaining and enforcing safety rules, procedures and behaviour guidelines
- Implementing tour arrangements
- Introducing tours and itineraries
- Guiding tourists round places of interest while giving appropriate commentary
- Safeguarding tourists safety throughout the tour
- Seeing guests onto and off coaches and other means of transport
- Establishing and maintaining friendly rapport with guests
- Answering guests' questions appropriately
- Supervising meal arrangements as necessary
- Managing problems arising on the tour so as to minimize their effect on the enjoyment of the tour
- Ensuring punctuality at all stages of the tour, time rules the job in tour guiding
- Adhering to the itinerary as closely as practicable
- Advising guests on use of free time
- Handling vouchers and cash transactions with sincerity on behalf of both the tourists and the tour operator
- Preparing and promptly submitting financial and tour reports to employers

- Advertising future tour opportunities or packages to tourists
- Sometimes preparing inexpensive souvenirs for tourists before, during or after the tour

Skills and competences of the tour guide

- The tour guide must have this wealth of skills and virtuous qualities:
- Maturity, intelligence, calmness
- vast knowledge, thoughtfulness, organised, time-conscious
- observant, good memory, safety conscious
- neat, tidy, smart appearance
- attention to details
- passionate interest in guiding
- genuine interest in people
- responsible and ability to take charge
- consideration for others
- good communication skills
- enduring (because the job is physically, vocally and psychologically challenging)
- Besides, the tour guide must constantly engage in research to update his/her knowledge
- Ability to say "I don't know"

Categories of Tour Guides

The Tour Guides' Association of Ghana (TORGAG) has categorised Ghanaian tour guides into six groups based on interest, training, competence and operational jurisdiction. One can train to become any of the following:

- Site guide
- Community/Local Guide
- Regional Guide
- National or General Guide
- Thematic or Specialist Guide
- Driver Guide

How does one become a Guide?

One can become a Tour guide by engaging in one or more of the following:

- In-service training: understudying an experienced practising tour guide on a bus, at a site, or during community tours.

- Informal training/Self-tuition: by reading on the subject and practising on the field.

- Formal training: pursuing a designated accredited guiding course from a recognized training institution. In Ghana, examples of training institutions include the Technical Universities, selected universities, professional institutions such as Hotel, Catering and Tourism Training Institute (HOTCATT).

The Tourism Phenomenon – Why are visitors coming?

Tourism

- is a voluntary, brief visit by people (from elsewhere) and involves travelling to new destinations (places)

- helps to share/or partake in experiences and activities at the destination (e.g. Sirigu)

- is the search of what will satisfy the needs of people namely physiological, social or psychological needs

Tourism invokes images of adventure, romance, mystery, exoticness, health therapy, study, culture, religion and VFR (visiting friends and relations).

Hence, our visitors want among other things, to relax, change from the routine, make new friends, learn new things, experience new cultures, and be happy within themselves.

This is where the tour guide comes in.

ASPECTS OF TOUR GUIDING

A. Physiological aspect of tour guiding

a) Guide's Appearance (checklist)

- Why is your appearance important? (Give the reasons)

- Grooming: involves body cleanliness, i.e. bathing, maintaining your mouth, hands, hair, clothes

- Proper bathing, using soap

- Clean, neat clothes/under-wears

- Neat, comfortable footwear, including socks

- Appreciable hairstyle, clean-shaven beard and moustache

- Appropriate dress for the occasion (example, to a shrine, forest, chief's palace, funeral, for climbing)

- Clean, neat handkerchiefs and hand tissue, hand sanitizers, mouthwash, nose masks as appropriate

- Judicious use of cosmetics, especially to cater for tourists who may be allergic to them and to remove you as the centre of focus to the tourists

- Decent and courteous mannerisms (no nose digging, indecent nose-blowing, spitting about)

- Frequent handwashing and freshening up

b) Poise, Voice and Communication

- Maintain the right physical and social distance, good but relaxing posture and genuinely smiling to your guests throughout the transaction

- Adopt flexible gestures: facial expression, eye-contact, appropriate body movement

- Be audible with or without microphone

- Check your tone, voice, inflection, volume, pitch, verbal pauses, pronunciation

- Use appropriate vocabulary, and explain local jargons

- Avoid gum-chewing, eating or drinking while guiding

- Avoid distractions such as playing with your phone

c) **Projected personality**

Radiate confidence, enthusiasm, friendliness and leadership. Be the ultimate "go-to" person for the tourist

B. Social aspects of tour guiding

- A pleasant rapport between you and the guests

- Incorporate relevant social and local cultural values into your presentation and encourage guests to have a sense of identifying with such values e. g. names of people, cultural titles, various forms of greetings (*Agoo, Miefon-a? Meda ase*)

- Use of anecdotes (e.g. childhood escapades) to embellish your presentation but be careful not to sway into the negative. Anecdotes may also help compare the past with the present to help bring out clearly societal evolution

C. Educational aspect of tour guiding

To fulfil the role of educating the guest, the tour guide must be versed in the wide array of subject areas and be able to successfully develop the subjects into meaningful and coherent "stories" for the tourist's appreciation.

The scope includes:

- **History**: ethnic history, migration, ethnic groups, foreign influence (including colonialism and missionaries), political history

- **Geography**: landscape, landforms, and related activities (biking, climbing, hiking), ancestral homes (e. g. caves),

- **Climate** and its relevance/conduciveness to tourist activities(weather, rainfall regimes, crop life, etc.)

- **Vegetation and related activities** (farming periods, farming methods, soil type, crop types, yields, contribution to local economy, promotional agricultural activities, etc.

- **Wildlife:** plants, animals and other living creatures, role in the economic and **spiritual life of the people**

- **Conservation modes** i.e. traditional methods (totems, sacred forests, and taboos), national parks, NGOs in conservation (e. g. Friends of Waterbodies, Green Earth Organisation, Wildlife Society)

- **Heritage, ethnic and living culture**

- **Ethnic groups and their spatial distribution**

- **Traditional institution**: family types, hierarchy, chieftaincy and related issues (i. e. selection, authority, enstoolment/enskinment of chiefs, regalia, palace courtesies, royal funerals)

- **Local festivals**: types of festivals, objectives, rituals and significance, ritual foods/dances, adornments, rites of passage, child naming and 'outdooring', Ghanaian names, etc.

- **Performing arts**: music, dances and ensembles (e.g. Borborbor, Agbadza, Adowa, Takai.), dancing costumes, occasions and times of performances, folktales, social values

- **Religious beliefs and institutions**: belief in God, cycle of man, death, reincarnation, ancestor veneration, libation prayer, shrines, churches, mosques, religious distribution, Fridays and "All-night" phenomenon

- **Health issues**: traditional and modern health systems, health management and administration, players in health service provision, infant mortality, maternal mortality, HIV/AIDS prevalence rate, infected population, interventions including ART (anti-retroviral) support, HIV/AIDS education (Recall the SDGs i.e. Sustainable Development Goals)

- **Political system**: traditional administration, constitutional democracy, decentralization/centralization, political role of the local authorities

- **Education system**: situation in the country/community with regards to informal education, formal education (policy), enrolment figures in school, duration, funding, government-civil society contributions, non-formal education (e. g. kayaye re-integration), employment and unemployment rate/figures, national service (refer to SDGs)

- **Socio-economic**: economic activities, income levels, daily income vis-à-vis daily minimum wage, inflation, tax regimes, energy/fuel issues (availability and prices), exports/imports, food security in the country/community, average family size, child-bearing, polygamy/monogamy issues, child-labour, children's rights, child trafficking, child dependency on parents and vice-versa, care for the aged, drug abuse, trafficking and related issues, crime wave, social life in the communities, homosexuality and same-sex marriage, abortion policy. **Note homosexuality, same-sex marriage and abortion are very sensitive areas which require great circumspection when discussing them.**

- **Local staples and cuisine** (i.e. food): method of cooking, occasions, how it is eaten

- **Local craft, dressing styles, myths and legends of the communities**

- **Markets** as economic centres and social rendezvous

- **Income generation and savings culture**: banking and investment, commercial banks, investment banks, (micro-) financial institutions, saving culture, investment opportunities

D. Ecological aspect of tour guiding

- **Immediate guiding environment**: Keep your community clean. Site guides must ensure neatness and orderliness of their halls, galleries, trails (refer to Afadjato, Paga pond, Tagbo and Nzulezo). Vehicle must be in order

- **General environmental/ecological issues:** Impact of activities on waterbodies, forests, mountains, Ghana's forest cover, deforestation and degradation activities including logging, farming, bush burning, bush-meat consumption, and chain-saw activities, mining and *galamsey* phenomenon

- **Positive community conservation practices**

  » Customary conservation methods: totems, sacred groves, deifying of natural features, sacred days ("da-bone" concept), periodic ban on farming and fishing activities

  » Statutory interventions: 11% of Ghana's land surface is under conservation with wetlands (Ramsar sites) along the coast to protect endangered species, community fire brigades, annual non-hunting season from 1st August to 1st December and ban on group hunting

- **Negative impact:** Bush burning, fuel wood, chain-saw logging, *"galamsey"* phenomenon, water-bodies/beach pollution, sand-winning along the beaches

- **Intervening institutions:** Wildlife Division, EPA (Environmental Protection Authority), NGOs, (e. g. Friends of Waterbodies, Green Earth Organisation, Ghana Wildlife Society etc.), local government, traditional authority

E. Safety aspect of tour guiding

- Operational information to guests: party control, road crossing, choice of stops, photo-taking protocol, avoiding dangerous areas, driver liaison, safe and comfortable driving

- Be circumspect in use of social media so as not to expose guests to preventable danger

- Watch out for criminals who may be trailing you.

- **Trust**: tourists want to see the guide as a genuine person who has integrity and can be trusted, one who can provide a reliable service in terms of the guest's welfare, assurance and commitment to the guest, punctuality and discipline (remember that time rules the business here)

- Provide adequate and accurate information and understanding of the places visited. To do this, the guide must draw a clear line between facts, legends and opinions and present information free from prejudice, bias and propaganda. He needs to protect and safeguard the reputation and rights of the destination and ensure that both the guest and the guide respect the values (e. g. dress protocol), local customs and sensitivities of the host community or country.

F. Psychological aspect of tour guiding

Tourists are happy when their self-esteem is boosted as they find it a privilege to be with a fantastic guide. They feel happy and proud of their travel decision. Elements that fulfill this desire include factual accuracy of presentations, good grasp of distances involved, confidence, selfless commitment, interesting and entertaining delivery, punctuality, presentable and well-groomed in personal care and hygiene.

G. Economic aspect of tour guiding

Value for money in respect of guiding and other services.

Note: The rule of thumb here is, as the Malaysians would say, to "receive the guests with smiles and send them off in tears"

Tours

a) Introducing tours

i. Always face the group to introduce tours, watch the space noting group size and observe necessary protocols e. g. Covid-19 protocols

ii. Greet guests appropriately, noting whether it is a formal, routine, casual or special occasion and the purpose. For example, *Agoo* and then introduce yourself clearly by name (official name first and foremost, and then add a name they should easily call you, hence the need to spell it out sometimes). Also refer to any peculiar feature (if appropriate) by which they can make you out at any given time during the tour. Another example, *Good morning, my name is Kwame; permit me to give you the program of the day…*

iii. Welcome guests, making references to their flight, previous night's sleep, journey to the community, etc.

iv. Give a brief information or outline of the tour/park/ site, highlighting for example the location, weather (recall Kintampo 2017 disaster), duration, main activities/ itinerary/ things to expect and so on. For example, *Feel relaxed, Ghanaians are very friendly and accommodating , this is the time to make a Ghanaian friend.*

v. Mention all others who may be with you on the tour, e.g. driver, hostess.

vi. Provide means of identification for each tourist especially if they are large in number

vii. Give any precautions they should take e.g. seatbelts for their own safety due to driving on a highway, washroom, dress, colour, touching, noise, pickpockets, Covid-19 protocols, non-swimming areas. Recall the fatal incident at Kintampo in March 2017 when a tree fell and killed seventeen students while swimming in the water.

viii. Stress the need for group cohesion and how *lost sheep* could be found

ix. Try to discover the party's interest and mood

x. Give opportunity for questions

xi. Thank guests and assure them of a pleasant tour. *Let's have a good time together!*

NOTE

1. You must always sound positive, encouraging and in control.

2. Avoid the tendency to memorize.

Commentary for critiquing

"Hello everyone, I'm your guide for today. I'll do my best to tell you all something about this city on our morning walk which will take us about 2 hours. So I hope your feet are in good shape; mine are killing me already, but then I've done this walk three times today already, and about 500 times before this! I'm sure you all remember some history about this city from your schooldays a long time ago. I was never good in history myself and even rotten at remembering dates. However, if you would like to listen for a while I'll try and tell you..." (Adapted from *Follow Me*)

Give a **detailed** critique and then write a better introduction of your own.

b) Coach Tours

- The driver is a very influential person on the coach. He has the ability to make or mar the tour. It is therefore essential that the tour guide gets on well with him and establishes a good working relationship. Remember the driver will discuss you with other drivers, which can help your reputation or put it at risk.

- Be in early to make sure that everything about the vehicle is alright: cleanliness, microphone adjusted to acceptable level, fuel, luggage racks, ventilation, emergency exits, necessary tools, fire extinguisher, toiletries, drinking water, etc. Remember that the tour guide is a leader and cannot say those aren't his responsibility.

- As far as possible, buy fuel when tourists are not on board. Do let the driver switch off the engine before you fill the tank. And remember to inform tourists before taking them to the gas or fuel station.

- Make sure you are familiar with the route and the pick-up points as you cannot guarantee that the driver is conversant with them. Identify loos or wash-rooms, cafes, restaurants and interesting items you may point out along the route (e.g. important buildings, specific trees or plants, water bodies, towns and some background information) and viewing points. It's important to get in first to check washrooms before guests go in to use them. It is professional to carry your own tissue and toiletries to forestall disappointment and embarrassment.

- Make stops for rest or washroom use at regular intervals, usually after two hours driving, or when requested by a guest.

- Check and note number in the group and regularly cross-check; you may use various techniques as appropriate to the group.

- Help visitors on and off the coach (unless the driver prefers to do it), but be sure that you obtain their approval before, because some may feel uncomfortable or embarrassed at such gestures.

- Sit in the courier seat beside the driver or just behind him so you can effectively communicate with him. If you have to stand, then be at the doorway (instep) so you don't block the view of your guests; they are not there to look at you.

- To begin the tour, introduce yourself and the driver, saying complimentary things about him to boost his morale as well as to give confidence to the group. Identify the coach. Face the group at this stage but not when the vehicle starts moving.

- Prayer may only be appropriate if the group is made up of ministers of God or if they are highly religious as may be with many Ghanaian groups. At best they may be asked to "silently commit the journey into the hands of their maker (or the Almighty)". Even if you have to pray on behalf of the group, be careful not to shout unnecessarily, or jump nor stamp your feet on the ground. Do not drag out.

- Point out features from where they can clearly see them, either before or whilst passing by them; not after you have passed by them. And remember that the vehicle is in motion at a certain speed. Effective liaison and cooperation with the driver are therefore very necessary.

- Mind the obvious and do not insult guests' intelligence, e.g. "this is a junction" when everyone can clearly see it already. Rather, what about the junction? Maybe there is something unique/peculiar/interesting about it. For example, *why Abavana Junction*?

- Where appropriate, stop for tourists to take pictures or to have a closer look at what you are describing. But give the driver advance notice; sudden stops don't only scare tourists but are really dangerous. Ensure that your conversation with the driver does not get to the rest of the group. The driver may also slow down for guests to clearly see what you are describing. Remember to obtain permission before touching or picking anything belonging to someone else but which you want to use for the tour.

- Make village stops where appropriate, e. g. Market day scenes, community activities, social performances, funerals. Over long stretches ("dead stretch") you may tell stories or discuss some aspects of our traditional culture, e.g. marriages, day names, festivals, inheritance, folk stories (Anansesem), educational system. Or sing a local song to break the monotony.

- Remember that a tour guide does not talk all the time. You need to study the group to know their mood and disposition. Appreciate that some groups need to be loaded with information whilst others prefer to observe more or engage in more interaction among themselves.

- After a session, tourists need time to absorb what you have said

- After lunch or on "dead stretches", tourists may want to observe, rest or snooze.

- You may prepare short notes usually in the form of shuffle cards or points, which you may refer to when you are not talking. Never read out a prepared script; it is not only unprofessional but may even mess you up

- When **one-third** is not listening, better stop talking or change the subject or your style; they either want to snooze or you may be boring

- If the group is the "know-all" type, adopt the interactive approach (that is, by involving or engaging them)

- Be specific which direction you are referring to, as your *left* may rather be their *right* depending on whether you are facing them or otherwise

- Do repeat guest questions for all to hear before you answer them

- Do not panic or get excited, but rather remain in control in any emergencies

- Give only background music and preferably indigenous music (except it is a general request from the group)

- Remind the driver when it's time for refreshment or lunch (and tips in some cases). The driver needs to be served early so he can have time to rest/snooze before he gets back behind the wheels.

- Never create the impression that there's some misunderstanding between the driver and you

- At hotels and restaurants, make sure that your tourists are comfortable. Always liaise with the tourists and staff and ensure the tourists get what they need. Remember, you can only think about your food when all your guests are sorted out.

- Never argue with tourists but you must be assertive

- Do not drink or smoke whilst on duty

- In case of vehicle breakdown, do arrange some activity to make them comfortable. Your maturity will come to play so much in problematic instances.

c) Walking Tours

- Could be done to waterfalls, mountains, in the forest, parks, within the village, city-centre

- It's useful to check the route every morning before tour begins

- Guests may have visited other attractions before yours, hence you must be very welcoming, entertaining, educative and ensure safety in order to make their coming worthwhile

- Remember to credit guests with some knowledge, do not insult their intelligence

- Adapt your presentations to suit each particular group (students, children, aged, religious groups), hence it's not useful to memorise

- Look out for what interests the group, but learn to judge their differences and resistance

- Walk at a leisurely pace so that guests can cope. Stop intermittently for guests to rest. You may coach them on how to climb easily.

- Gather group and face them anytime you want to give commentary (unless group comprises just 1 or 2 persons)

- Choose stopping locations carefully, mindful of their safety, comfort and other pedestrians

- Draw guests' attention to dangers (open drains, hanging trees, thorns, ants) and actually help them get through such challenges; do not take things for granted.

- Indicate clearly what you are describing (by use of hand, appropriate descriptive words)

- Answer guest questions to the benefit of all, don't be involved with just a few but do give much attention to those who need special attention (e.g. weak ones)

- Stay cool and in control in any emergencies, never panic nor get excited

- As appropriate, use human anecdotes about the site, to make the tour lively as well as stress the importance of the sites or resource e.g. childhood climbing episodes, folk-stories related to the forest, palm-wine tapping and efforts to control bush fires

- Encourage your guests to minimise their negative impact on the resource or environment, and to take home a conservation message

- Your presentation should relate to global or universal conservation concerns, e.g. themes such as food, shelter, family life

- Welcome guests back after the tour and invite any questions they may have

- Introduce them to any souvenirs/gift shops to purchase memorabilia

- Thank them for their co-operation and express the

hope that they will come again

- Bid them good-bye

d) Guest Transfer/Collection

Guest Transfers require:
- Neat, decent, comfortable and well-maintained vehicles, free of mosquitoes and other insects

- Punctuality: be at airport or pick-up point at least 30 to 60 minutes before scheduled arrival time given

- Observe all driving and parking rules and details at the pick-up points. Note that picking guests at unauthorised points do not only attract quite high fines but can also be embarrassing and demoralizing and sometimes stressful to guests

- Ensure there are toiletries, insecticides, sanitizers, Dettol in the vehicle (especially for sightseeing excursions)

- Employ identification techniques for guests to recognize you but be mindful of swindlers or crooks at the ports and tourist points. Usually, use a tag or a boldly printed out signboard for easy identification by guests, but no loose disclosure of guest details to others around

- When guest arrives, greet warmly to encourage positive feelings of goodwill

- Check and note number of baggage pieces, ensuring that guests have brought out all their baggage items. Follow established procedures for lost baggage

- Provide guests with adequate information or advice on cultural sensitivities of destination, including currency, money exchange rates, forex bureaus, time-change, weather as appropriate

- Brief guests on accommodation arrangements

- Do liaise and minimise communication difficulties between visitors and other officials and staff

Note that your role is to endeavour to remove all likely bottlenecks.

e) Basic Traffic control guidelines

- Undertaking walking tours in towns and city-centres will require the tour guide to engage in some basic traffic management to ensure guest safety as well as the success of the tour. This is in cognizance of the fact that vehicles as well as other users share the roads and highways with the tourists.

- This role is more prominent in the peculiar circumstance of our cities and towns as some sections lack designated pavement or sidewalk and marked crossings. Compounding the problem further is the absence and/or scanty knowledge of bicycle lanes as against pedestrian lanes.

- Traditionally, we face on-coming vehicles, remembering that we drive on the right in Ghana. However, absence of walkways or pavements along certain routes may compel us to ignore this rule.

- Road-signs and traffic indicators are those accepted internationally and may include zebra crossing or markings, traffic lights, the Triangle, among others. We must however remember to take cognizance of the indigenised (non-conventional) methods sometimes adopted by drivers on our roads (e.g. use of fresh leaves in place of the Triangle in some cases in Ghana).

- A Tour Guide must essentially obey all traffic regulations and therefore employ the road signs and designations when undertaking a tour. Crossings must therefore be done at authorised points such as traffic lights, zebra crossings, near roundabouts and at points where road management officers such as the Police can facilitate easy crossing.

- In situations where it is practically impossible to have access to the above, the following steps must be observed when crossing the road with your group:

  » Group together by the point where you want to cross

  » Be patient and stay calm and watch out for a break in traffic

  » When there's a break in traffic, take a step into the road with your left hand raised, make sure the driver sees you i.e. "eye-to-eye". Anticipate well the speed of the next vehicle before you step into the road.

  » With your hand still raised straight up, stand in the middle of the road when the driver stops for you, or when road is still clear and ask the group to cross

  » Stand there until the last person crosses

  » If it is a dual carriage road, instruct group to wait at the 'island' for you to join them.

> » After the last person has crossed, thank the driver and leave the road

- At intersections and roundabouts, do not cross too close to the circle; cross some 15 metres away from the circle.

- Never adopt jaywalking in crossing the road

- Do look out for open drains, exposed electric wires and other dangers and direct your guests accordingly

f) Service Value Sought/Felt by Customers

1. Wonder/Marvel

Exceeding guest expectations by way of pleasant surprises, weighted suggestions, anticipation of needs

2. Security/Trust

Insight and sensitivity, Empathy, Consistency

3. Friendliness/Resourcefulness

Friendliness and sense of fellowship, genuine smiling face, flexible adaptability, presentable appearance

4. Business Uprightness and Basic Handling

Adequate information, accuracy, promptness/punctual responsiveness, good listening, Gratitude and apologies, Follow-up

NB: Remember that the tourist may already have an 'image bag' before coming.

g) Some Dos and Don'ts on the Tour

- It's advisable to deal with the leader of the group

- Never give the impression of any misunderstanding between your colleagues and you. Avoid an argument with a guest, be assertive though but not aggressive (e.g. *I appreciate your efforts but I am in charge.*

- Don't frown upon questions as they tend to rather help elucidate your presentations

- Never drink nor chew gum whilst on duty

- Be careful not to treat disabled people differently but with dignity as with others, e.g. do not treat a disabled adult as if he or she is a child; do not tap him or her on the back as you speak with the guest

- Avoid leaning or hanging onto a person's wheelchair

- Don't assume that people in wheelchairs need to be pushed necessarily; always find out before offering help

- If you do help move a person in a wheelchair, do not leave him or her in a dangerous place (e.g. slope)

- If you lead a person with poor vision by the hand, do not try to push or pull the person; rather, give him or her clear instructions as necessary

- For one who cannot see at all, or sees very poorly, do identify yourself and anyone else with you

- Do speak slowly but expressively to those with hearing difficulty

- For guests with difficulty in speaking, do be patient and encouraging. Do not try to correct nor take over what he or she is trying to say. You may ask short questions, particularly close questions when appropriate.

h) Some Frequently Asked Questions by Visitors

- **HIV/AIDS**: rate of prevalence, infected population, interventions including ART, stigmatization, support and education

- **Health policies and systems:** cost, health insurance, herbal and alternative medicine, spiritual and psychic healing

- **Education:** prevailing system at various levels of education: duration, enrolment figures and percentage in school, tuition fees and other expenditure, boarding/day system, National service, employment/unemployment figures (rates)

- **Socio-economic**: economic activities, income levels, daily minimum wage, rate of inflation, average family size, polygamy/monogamy issues, birth-rate/death-rate, child labour, children dependency on parents and vice-versa, aged homes, religious composition and activities, energy (electricity) generation, consumption and tariffs, women/child rights, accommodation and prices of buildings, communication and internet access, drug trafficking and abuse and related issues, crime wave, cigarette smoking, drug use, Ghana-China relations (mainly from Americans), Ghana's view on American elections (if election year), Ghana's economy vis-à-vis global challenges,

- **Major export products/commodities:** e.g. the carats of gold mined in Ghana/price of one gram

- **Trading partners**

- **Methods of disposing dead bodies:** burial or cremation

Note that some of the areas can be sensitive and thus require a great deal of circumspection in answering them e.g. homosexuality/gayism, atheism/deism, abortion.

NB: As a technique to prepare adequately for a tour, the route must be segmented to make it easier in identifying landmarks and interesting things to mention on the tour. For example, Accra-Cape Coast tour could be segmented into Accra-Kasoa, Kasoa-Winneba, Winneba-Mankesim and Mankesim-Cape Coast.

a) History and cultural development of the community

- Historical background and development of the community: origin/migration, meaning of name
- Cultural traits of the community: food types and mode of preparation, -mode of walking (at old age), talking, dancing, e.t.c.
- Folklore and entertainment: e.g. Anansesem (Glitoto among the Ewe), proverbs, indoor games, dirges
- Traditional costumes/attires and their value to the people
- Festivals and rites: e.g. Bakatue, Dipo, funerals
- When and how they are celebrated/performed?
- Who takes part?
- Unique elements/things about the festivals
- Significance of festival to the community (and nation)
- Rites: marriage, child-naming, out-dooring, puberty, funerals, significance of rituals
- Religious beliefs: ancestral reverence, libation (prayer), sacrifice and offering
- Customary law

b) Oral presentations on chosen topics to visitors, things to look out for

- Presenter's Appearance
- Ability to arouse interest and enthusiasm in guests

- Appropriateness of commentary for the audience

- Appropriate choice of words/language

- Ability to encourage belief and understanding

- Good control of questions

- Audibility, countenance (relaxed, smiling, eye-contact)

c) Practical guiding checklist

- Guide's Appearance

- Projected personality, enthusiasm, confidence, pleasant rapport

- Driver liaison (in the case of coach tours)

- Safety and operational information to visitors e.g. precautions, group control

- Audibility, clarity of speech, accurate expressions

- Appropriate sightings and timings

- Relevance of commentary to clients/or circumstances

- Factual accuracy

- Interesting, entertaining, anecdotal

- Good handling of questions

ENGLISH WORDS AND PHRASES
American English vs. English (UK)
English nuances

It is useful to note the nuances in some words and terminologies as used by the British and the Americans. This will help the tour guide in dealing appropriately with groups of English or American backgrounds.

British English	*American English*
pavement/footpath	sidewalk
fuel (station)	gas (station)
flat	apartment
bill (at restaurant)	check (at restaurant)
(form) a queue	(form) a line
lift	elevator
chemist/pharmacy	drugstore
trousers	pants
toilet/loo/cloakroom	restroom/comfort station
packed lunch	sack lunch
timetable	schedule
holiday	vacation
receptionist	desk clerk

tap (water)	faucet (water)
black/white coffee/tea	(tea/coffee) with or without milk
nought/zero	zero
articulated lorry	trailer truck
caravan	trailer
single ticket	one-way ticket

TOURISM AND THE UN SUSTAINABLE DEVELOPMENT GOALS: (SDGS) 2016 – 2030

The Tour guide must be abreast with the SDGs and relate the relevant aspects to his/her operations. It is therefore important to note the following goals that are pertinent to tourism and for that matter, tour guiding.

- Goal 9: Innovation and Infrastructure – Status and programmes in the hinterland and in tourism enclaves

- Goal 11: Sustainable cities – Cities and infrastructural planning, pollution

- and disaster prevention, population growth and density

- Goal 12: Sustainable Consumption and Production – Industries and impact on cities, tourism regulation, capacity planning at the tourist sites

- Goal 13: Combat climate change – Efforts, education and activities to stem climate

- change (impact) in the system, contribution to CFCs

- Goal 14: Save the Oceans, Seas and Marine World – Regulation of fishing, garbage dumping, protection of endangered species, wetlands management

- Goal 15: Save the Forests – Afforestation moves, reduction on exploitation of the forest (fuel wood, lumbering and sawing), protected areas, bushfires

SOME RELEVANT GUIDING AND TOURISM TERMINOLOGIES

Day trip: A return trip on the same day and therefore does not involve spending the night at the destination.

Overnight trip: A trip that involves sleeping over at the destination.

Single occupancy: A hotel room paid for and slept in by one person.

Double occupancy: A hotel room slept and paid for by 2 persons. It can be a twin room or a double room.

Shared accommodation: means the same as double occupancy.

Supplement: An extra or additional amount paid by a guest for extra service or upgrade of facilities over and above the published fee or price. Supplements are mainly related – though not restricted – to accommodation. Hence, there could be single occupancy supplement, seaview/ocean view supplement, baby cot supplement.

Transfer: Meeting, welcoming and leading guests from point of entry to arranged accommodation, or from hotel to port of departure, e.t.c. This is otherwise referred to as "meet and greet" service.

Continental breakfast: Beverage (tea or coffee) + carbohydrate (bread, toast or rolls) + butter, jam and marmalade (sometimes with juice).

English breakfast: Tea or coffee, juice and/or cereal, toast, main dish (of fish or meat or a combination), butter and preserves. It is a more elaborate breakfast.

Bed and breakfast: Includes accommodation and breakfast (Continental breakfast or English breakfast).

Halfboard (MAP or demi-pension): inclusive price for room, breakfast and one main meal each day.

Fullboard (AP or enpension): Inclusive price for room plus 3 meals a day (i. e. breakfast, lunch and dinner).

Itinerary: A description of a tour, outlining the sequence of travel, routing (route), distances involved, travel dates and times, places to be visited, and the activities to be undertaken, and sometimes the mode of transport.

Tour package: A combination of travel services (e.g.: transfer, accommodation, meals, etc.) sold together to a client at an inclusive or single price

Inclusive price: The price at which a tour package comprising specified services is sold.

PART TWO

GHANA-SPECIFIC TOUR INFORMATION

INTRODUCTION

This part tackles some essential information that are relevant in guiding guests around Ghana. It dwells on information that may, by anticipation and experience, be very useful in meeting the education aspect of guiding as you conduct guests around Ghana. A caveat, though, is that every country is dynamic and therefore some information, particularly socio-economic indicators, may change from time to time. Hence, there is need for periodic research and updates in order to be efficient and effective. It is also important to remember that in tour guiding, "one plus one is not necessarily two." You must therefore know that you cannot be necessarily accurate in certain instances but to use estimation, approximation, comparison or, at best, draw on personal experience.

For example, how would you answer the question from a guest as to the weight of a load a woman from the farm is carrying when you have not weighed it? Or how much money does a road-side peanut seller make in a day when you have not spoken to her to find out?

It is also important to note that you do not impress a guest by providing a wrong answer. He may find out sooner than later that you lied. It is better to genuinely acknowledge that you do not know (and that you may find out later, if that is practicable). But hey, that should not be the norm as to end up being christened "Mr. or Ms. I-don't-know".

Another instance where you don't need to be exact but to approximate is to avoid confusing your guests with 'bulky' figures. It is more difficult for your guest to remember, for example, that Ghana covers a surface area of 239,460sq. km than to round it up to 240,000sq. km. This is when the words **about** or **approximately** will be useful. You can therefore say "Ghana is approximately 240,000sq. km" for effect, understanding and appreciation. Approximation also settles inherent discrepancies or controversies; for example, whether Ghana's area is 238,460sq. km. or 239,460sq. km.

A personal advice is for all tour guides to re-visit their knowledge of basic arithmetic indicators such as mile-kilometre equivalence, how to describe distance in terms of metre-kilometre, and when to differentiate between distance and area as well as to correctly approximate distance when on the road.

Example: 1000m = 1km, 1km = 0.625mile, 1mile = 1.6km

BRIEF GEOGRAPHY OF GHANA

1. LOCATION AND AREA

Ghana
- lies between 4° and 11° N and 1° E and 3° W

- Is crossed by the Greenwich Meridian at Tema

- Has an area of 239, 460 sq. km (92,000 sq. miles)

2. RELIEF / TOPOGRAPHY

A. Lowlands

i) Coastal Plains

- Starts from around Sekondi, extending north-east through Central Region, Greater Accra to Southern Volta Region

- Very broad (80km) in the east and west but narrow between Winneba and Accra (16km)

- Sub-classified into Accra Plains, plains west of Accra, and the coastline,

  » Accra Plains – South-East Coastal plains, fairly flat with isolated hills (inselbergs) e.g. Shai Hills, Osudoku Hills, Krobo Hills, Ningo Hills. General elevation is around 75m a.s.l. (above sea level) with Keta area below sea level. (Recall the Sea Defense Project)

  » West of Accra is undulating land with isolated steep hills

  » Coastline: 540km stretch of sandy coast with about 50 lagoons

» Mostly smooth coast with sand bars, but cliffed in some areas such as James town, Abandze, and Komenda

ii) Voltain Sandstone Basin

- Covers almost half of Ghana's land surface: 112.768sq. km

- Area mostly drained by Volta Lake and tributaries of River Volta

- Average elevation is between 60m and 150m a.s.1. (200 – 500ft)

B. Highlands

i)   Akwapim-Togo Ranges

- A chain of fold mountains

- Forms the Eastern boundary of Volta basin

- Runs north-east from the mouth of River Densu through the Eastern Region, across the Volta Region into Togo, Benin and the Niger Valley

- Average height is between 600m and 800m

- Highest point is Afadjato at 885m (2,905ft)

- Other mountains on the range include Gemi (762m), Agumatsa (840m), Avegbadjie (863m), Torogbani (872m) and Djebobo (875m)

NOTE: **GEMI** stands for German Evangelical Missionary Institute.

ii)   Southern Volta Plateau (Kwahu Plateau)

- Marks the Southern boundary of the Volta basin

- Average elevation of 450m-500m

- Runs Southeast to northwest

- Series of escarpments, with South-facing scarps known as Kwahu (Nkawkaw) scarp

- Mountains include Atiwa-Atwiradu (738m), Akwawa (788m), Ejuanema (744m) where annual Paragliding event is held during Easter.

iii)   Forest dissected plateau (Mampong Scrap)

- Average height between 300 and 400m

- Lies within heavy rainfall area

- Hence heavy vegetation prevents sheet erosion leading to plateau being heavily dissected

- Many rivers and streams take their source from the area e.g. Tano, Afram, Sene, Offin, Pru

iv)   Gambaga (Nakpanduri) Scarp

- Runs east-west in northeast Ghana

- Forms the Northern end of the Volta Basin,

- Average height of 450m

v) Savannah high plains:

- Spread across Western part of Northern Region and north-western part of Upper East and Upper West Region

- Average height of 180m-300m

3. DRAINAGE

- Volta River is the largest and longest (1600km long). The river is dammed at Akosombo resulting in the creation of the Volta Lake upstream

- The Volta Lake covers about 8480sq. km, i.e. from Yapei in the north to Akosombo in the south

- Together with its tributaries, the Volta River drains 67% of the country

- The main tributaries include Black Volta, Red Volta, White Volta, Oti (all taking their source in Burkina Faso). The other tributaries of the Volta are Afram, Sene, Kulpawn, and Nasia.

- Middle portion of the Volta River is now a lake following its damming at Akosombo in early 1960s

- Other important rivers in Ghana are Tano, Ankobra, Pra, Birim, Densu, and Ayensu

- Many of the rivers flow into the sea

- Lake Bosumtwi is the largest natural lake in Ghana and is inland drainage. It covers an area of about 50sq. km, surrounded by hills 500m in elevation. Its origin is traced to a meteoric impact (though some link it to a volcanic activity)

- The Volta Lake is man-made, 415km long and covering approximately 8480sq.km from Yapei to Akosombo. Its construction resulted in the displacement of 700 communities with 52 resettlement towns built in 1956/57. Some of the re-settled towns are New Senchi, Katanga and Asukawkaw

4. CLIMATE

- Tropical climate

- Temperature range in the south is between 21°C and 34°C, and 24°C and 40°C in the north. Average daily temperature in Ghana is 29°C

- Warmest months are February and March, and coolest month is August

- Two rainfall regimes in the south: Major wet season is April -June and minor wet season is September-October

- One wet season in the north from May to August

- Annual rainfall ranges between 3020mm in the south-west and 762mm on the Accra plains as well as in Navrongo area

5. VEGETATION

i)   Mangrove Swamp Forest

- In the lagoons, brackish and tidal water, trees with stilt root, average height of 17m

- Fresh –water swamp forest with raffia palms found inland and around Nzulezu area

ii)   Coastal Savanna

Found between rain forest and the sea

- Comprises of dense scrub in the west and grassland in the east

- Occasional trees, particularly baobab, are found in the Accra Plains. Other trees include neem and mango trees

iii)   Tropical Rainforest

- Found in the south-west corner of Ghana

- High temperatures and heavy rainfall year round

- Dense, luxuriant, evergreen forest

- Forest has 3 distinct layers

- Trees grow straight, reaching up to 70m high

- Sparse undergrowth, with mosses, epiphytes and woody climbers

iv) Moist Semi-Deciduous Forest

- Covers much of central Ghana (Ashanti, Eastern, Central, part of Volta, Oti and Brong Ahafo)

- Annual rainfall ranges between 1270mm and 1800mm

- Dry season is more pronounced than in the tropical rainforest zone

- Most of Ghana's valuable timber trees namely Odum, Mahogany, Cedar and Sapele are found in this zone

- Semi-deciduous characteristics of trees in upper and middle tiers, thus shedding their leaves during long dry season (November-March)

- The main forest vegetation that supports cocoa production in the country

v) Savannah Grassland

- Covers northern half of the country

- Mainly grass with scattered trees

- Taller grasses and bigger trees in the transition zone

- Trees adapted to withstand dry season: they have small leaves, thick barks and deep roots to tap water.

- Most trees shed leaves during the dry season

- Trees mainly include baobab, acacia, shea and dawadawa

6. POLITICAL, POPULATION AND ECONOMIC

Indicators and indices are very much susceptible to change. The highly elastic nature of these indicators does not make it prudent to capture figures in this book. Instead, the various areas of interest and concern have been listed so as to guide users and readers to look out for the appropriate yearly data and figures.

Country has **16** administrative regions:
- Greater Accra Region (GAR) 3245km²

- Central Region (CR) 9,826 km²

- Eastern Region (ER) 19,323 km²

- Ashanti Region (ASR) 24,389 km²

- Western and Western North Regions (WR & WNR) 23,921 km²

- Volta and Oti Regions (VR & OtiR) 20,570 km²

- Bono, Ahafo and Bono East Regions (BNR, AHR & BER) 39,557 km²

- Northern, Savannah and North-East Regions (NR, SVR & NER) 70,384km²

- Upper East region (ER) 8842 km²

- Upper West Region (UWR) 18476 km²

- 260 administrative districts (as at June 2020)

- 275 constituencies (as at 2019)

- About 67 major and minor ethnic groups with about 47 languages

- Population

- Population density (per km²)

- Regional population distribution

- Male-female distribution

- Age distribution

- Adult population

- Urban/rural population

- Birth/Death rate

- Infant mortality rate

- Life expectancy

- Literacy rate

- HIV/AIDS prevalence rate

- Size of economy

- Economic growth rate

- Inflation rate

- Income status of country

- Per capita income

- Daily minimum wage

- Joblessness/unemployment rate/figures

- Economic sectors: Services, Industry, agriculture

- Informal sector employment

- Formal sector employment

- Energy production and consumption

- Solid waste generation and treatment

- Transport and Communication: roads, rail, air, tele-density

- Seaports: Takoradi (1928) and Tema (1962)

- Ghana's Trade partners

- Ghana is a secular country with guaranteed freedom

of religion comprising: Christians, Traditionalists, Moslems, Others, No religion

7. MAJOR LANGUAGES

- English (as official language)
- Akan
- Ewe
- Ga-Adangbe
- Dagbani
- Gonja
- Guan

COLONIAL & POLITICAL HISTORY OF GHANA

Charles McCarthy

- British military officer of Irish and French ancestry

- Arrived to be Governor in 1821 from Sierra Leone where he was Governor

- He declared war on Ashanti after fighting to protect the castle at Cape Coast

- In 1824, organised different British allies and marched towards Kumasi

- Was killed and beheaded during an ambush near Bonsaso, on the river Bonsa which runs into the Ankobra river

George Maclean

- Was in the Gold Coast from 1831 to 1843

- Was in charge of British interests (forts) in the Gold. Coast

- Was not to meddle in local state affairs, sought harmonious relationships with the locals

- He signed a peace treaty with the Ashanti in 1831

- He had a court in Cape Coast Castle in which judgement was mostly according to Akan custom

Bond of 1844 (6th March 1844)

- Signed between Commander Hill and some coastal chiefs (seven initially but later ten others joined)

- The Bond regularized relations with the locals living along the coast. It turned out (according to Professor Albert Adu-Buahen) to be the first major imperial assault on the rights and powers of coastal Gold Coasters to administer their own affairs

- The Bond outlawed certain customary practices (e.g. human sacrifices and *panyarring*)

- Criminal cases were to be tried by British officials in conjunction with the chiefs

- Overall, the locals were to be under British protection for 100 years

- The Second World War disrupted this arrangement as everybody was pre-occupied by the war

- The Document therefore started the process of consolidating British power, authority, and jurisdiction which was concretized in 1874 by an Act in British Parliament

- Signatories to the Bond include Chiefs of Denkyira, Abora, Dominase, Assin, Anomabu, and Cape Coast and later by ten others, namely Twifo, Ekumfi, Jamestown, Gomoa, Agona Nsaba, Wassa Amenfi, Wassa Fiase, Asikuma, Dixcove and Ajumako

Poll Tax Ordinance (1852)

- A direct tax introduced in 1852 by Commander Hill

- Objective was to help provide amenities and development such as schools, hospitals etc. for the people

- Yearly tax of one shilling (or 15 cowries) by each person of every household, including children

- Chiefs were used to collect the tax

- Discontent and agitations culminating in the Christiansborg rebellion of 1854

<u>Reasons for refusal to pay</u>

a. Paying the tax every year was just too much

b. The people claimed they were poor and could not pay

c. Chiefs had no right to accept the imposition of the tax on their behalf

d. Dishonesty on the part of some of the tax collectors

e. Development not commensurate with the tax being collected

<u>Result</u>

- Bombardment and destruction of Teshie and La (Labadi). Hundreds of people were killed. The poll tax was abolished in **1861.**

Fante Confederacy (1867-1872)

- Fante and other coastal chiefs met at Mankesim (*Omankesie*) to form a confederacy to, among other things, help Komenda in their military resistance against the Dutch as well as speed up the development of their area

- The Confederacy was short-lived as it collapsed in 1873. Just before then, their confederation army was used to fight along the side of Komenda and Dixcove against the Dutch in the aftermath of the swapping of forts under the "Sweet river" agreement

- The Confederacy's Coat of Arms of a palm tree behind an elephant was later adopted by the colonial government until independence

Swapping of Forts (British and Dutch), 1867

For economic prudence, the remaining colonial powers in the Gold Coast (i.e. the British and the Dutch) decided in 1867 to each group their forts together and

a. Charge the same customs rate to check smuggling and unnecessary rivalry. So in 1867 the Dutch gave their forts in Moree, Kormantse, Apam (Patience) and Crevecoeur (Ussher) to the British and in turn assumed ownership of the British forts in Beyin (Appollonia), Dixcove (Metal Cross), British Komenda and Sekondi (Ft. Orange).

- **Sweet River** became the boundary with all property east of the river belonging to the British and the property west of the river now being for the Dutch.

- Komenda was bombarded (by a Dutch war ship) because the locals had refused to accept them as their new masters; the former had all this while aligned with the British against the Asante and the Dutch. The Denkyira then blocked the Dutch trade route to the coast.

- In 1872 the Dutch sold their property to the British and left the Gold Coast to take over British property in Java, Indonesia.

Sagrenti War of 1872-1874

- In 1872, Adu Bofo of Asante captured three European missionaries and one European merchant

- Asantehene demanded a ransom for the release of the captives. He wanted 1800 ounces (112.5pds) of gold, but the British governor was ready to pay less. The Asante additionally asked for free access to Elmina Castle to trade

- The events led to the Sagrenti War of 1874 (led by Sir Garnet Wolseley on the British side). The Asante were defeated by the British who had reinforced their troops with 2000 white soldiers plus soldiers from Sierra Leone and Nigeria. It was during this war that the British burnt Kumasi and destroyed the Asantehene's palace at Adum

- Asantehene (now) was requested in the treaty of Fomena to pay 50,000 ounces of gold to the British, give up trading control over Denkyira, Assin, Akyem and Elmina, open up the territory to the British for trade, and abolish human sacrifices

- Asantehene could only pay 1,000 ounces and therefore had to be arrested by the British in 1896. They took him into Elmina Castle for four years and then exiled him to the Seychelles Island in the Indian Ocean for 24 years.

Note: The Asante fought the British in nine **bloody** wars, the last one being the Yaa Asantewa War of 1900.

The British Protectorate

On 24 July 1874 the British formally declared southern Gold Coast a Crown Colony covering all states south of the river Pra.

Lands Bill of 1897

This bill proposed to vest all vacant lands in the Queen of the United Kingdom. Drawing from experiences in Kenya, the Aborigines Rights Protection Society (ARPS) was formed to contest the bill. It was later withdrawn following protestations and a presentation made to the Queen by members of the ARPS.

Already, there have been earlier challenges to the British authority in the Gold Coast following the Bond of 1844 and subsequent developments. Prominent challengers include Kwadwo Tsibu of Denkyira, Kwaku Ackah of Nzema and John Aggrey – Chief of Cape Coast, who was the first Gold Coaster to be exiled to Sierra Leone for championing the cause of self-determination.

Yaa Asantewa War

Governor Hodgson had demanded to sit on the Golden Stool, but Yaa Asantawa resisted it, triggering the Yaa Asantewa War of 1900.

Annexation of Asante and northern territories

- 1901: Asante was annexed as part of the British colony following the former's defeat in the war: the northern territories were also declared a British protectorate

- Main reasons for the annexation of the northern territories were to **(i)** consolidate British presence in the Gold Coast, **(ii)** prevent the French and Germans from making further incursions into northern parts of the

Gold Coast and **(iii)** suppress the threats and activities of the slave raiders (Babatu, Samori and Bagao).

- Note that Bagao was captured in 1905 and executed by firing squad thanks to the British authorities then stationed at Gambaga. Samori had been taken prisoner by the French in 1899. Babatu was alleged to have died in Yendi.

Trans-Volta Togoland (1921)

Trans-Volta Togoland became an adjunct of the Gold Coast following the defeat of Germany in the 1st World War

European Goods Boycott

Nii Kwabena Bonne III led the national boycott of European goods in late 1940s.

AWAM (Association of West African Merchants)

There was scarcity of so-called essential goods e.g. sugar and milk, leading to high inflation in the Gold Coast immediately after the 2nd World War. The thinking then was that the colonialists and Lebanese merchants had deliberately orchestrated the shortage. Hence the decision to boycott their products.

UGCC (United Gold Coast Convention)

The first political party in the Gold Coast was formed in August 1947 in Saltpond at the Canaan Lodge, a property of Mr. Albion Mends (the first postmaster of Gold Coast) who was the Treasurer of UGCC with Paa Grant as the sole financier.

The Big Six

Arrest and imprisonment of UGCC leaders accused of being behind the 1948 riots. These six men became known later in our political parlance as the **"Big Six"**.

Crossroad Shooting Incident

Happened on 28 February 1948. Gunning down of three ex-servicemen following a peaceful march by disillusioned ex-service men to present a petition to the Governor at Christiansborg Castle. The reasons for that move included the following, among others:

- Failure of the government to resettle the ex-servicemen

- Shortage of accommodation for the ex-soldiers

- shortage and concomitant high prices of essential commodities

- Increasing unemployment among the youth

- The surge of swollen shoot disease and the government's suggested solution to farmers to cut down affected cocoa trees

- The shooting and killing of three ex-servicemen on

28th February 1948 served as the immediate cause that triggered the 1948 riots. The riots led to looting of shops in Accra and other centers such as Nsawam, Somanya and Koforidua.

Remember that the 2nd World War had demystified the white man and had raised the self-esteem of the black man.

Convention People's Party (CPP)

- Nkrumah left the UGCC to form the CPP (Convention People's Party) in June 1949

- 1951: Nkrumah became Leader of Government Business following victory for CPP in the 1951 elections.

- 1952: Nkrumah became Prime Minister

Independence

Declaration of independence on 6th March, 1957 at the old Polo Grounds (hitherto a no-go area for the locals).

Post-Independence

- 1st July 1960: Ghana declared a republic with Nkrumah as the 1st President.

- 1966 – 2020: Political mix-grill: NLC, PP, NRC, SMC 1, SMC 2, AFRC, PNP, PNDC, NDC, NPP, NDC, NPP

- 1992 to date: 4th Republican Constitution that has resulted in a stable multi-party democracy so far

- Fl. Lt. Jerry John Rawlings who is credited with the introduction of the 4th Republican Constitution died on 12 November 2020 at age 73. He served as the first President (from 7th January 1992 to 6th January 2001) under the 4th Republican Constitution of Ghana.

EUROPEAN PRESENCE IN THE GOLD COAST

- In their attempt to find a new sea-route to the Far East, Europeans came into contact with West Africa and started trading with the region in gold, cotton, gum, ivory, parrots and other live-animals. The Europeans, in return, offered the Africans items such as brass and metal wares, mirrors, woven fabrics and ready-made clothing, liquor, beads, guns and gunpowder and animal hides.

- The Europeans began trading and exporting slaves towards the end of the 16th Century i.e. the Trans-Atlantic Slave Trade. The Slave Trade was abolished by Great Britain in 1807, followed by abolishing of slavery in the British Empire in 1833. (Recall that the practice of pawning and other forms of servitude among early indigenous people of present-day Ghana was different.)

- The Portuguese were the first to arrive in the Gold Coast in 1471. They opened a gold mine at Abrobi (mina der ouri) near Komenda. They later built the Elmina Castle and trading forts at Axim, Shama and Accra. They left the Gold Coast following the Dutch capture of the Elmina Castle from them in 1637.

- The Dutch arrived in 1593 and first settled at Mori where they built a trading fort in 1598. Following their capture and seizure of the St. George's Castle in 1637, they consolidated their presence by building more forts including Forts William (Anomabu), Patience (Apam), Good Hope (Senya Breku), Orange (Sekondi) and Crevecoeur/Ussher (Accra). They left the Gold Coast for good in 1872 having sold their properties in the Gold Coast to the British.

- Other Europeans present in the Gold Coast prior to the latter's declaration of independence include the English who built their first fort at Kormantse in 1631. They were the last to pull out of Gold Coast following the regaining of independence by the latter.

- The Danes were present in Cape Coast, Ada, Nungua, Teshie, Osu and Keta. The Danes also introduced plantation farming in the Gold Coast, specifically in Accra and Akwapim. They left the Gold Coast in 1850 having sold their possessions to the British for 10,000 pounds. The Swedes were present at Amanful, Osu, and Cape Coast. The Brandenburgers arrived in 1681 and built forts in Princestown (town named after Prince Wilhem 1 of Prussia), and two others in the Western region.

- By the turn of the 19th Century, about 50 buildings comprising castles, forts and lodges had been built by Europeans in the Gold Coast for use as either

-   a) trading posts, ware-house facilities and for security,

-   b) living quarters for a permanent commercial and military staff

Note: at the very early stages, the Europeans did not have any territorial jurisdiction beyond the walls of their castles or forts.
- The castles and forts were concentrated along the stretch of the Gold Coast due to the following reasons:

a. Existence of substantial gold deposits comparatively near the coast

a. Rocky coast which provided building materials and

natural strong foundations

a. Existence of natural harbours along Ghana's coast

- Some of the European forts and settlements in the Gold Coast include the following:

Axim (Fort St. Anthony)	Portuguese	1515
Butre (Ft. Batenstein)	Portuguese/Swedes/Dutch	1650/1656
Shama (Ft. San Sebastian)	Portuguese/Dutch	1526/1640
Kormantse (Ft. Amsterdam)	English/Dutch	1638
Senya Breku (Ft. Good Hope)	Dutch	1705
Apam (Ft. Patience)	Dutch	1697-1702
Anomabu (Ft. William)	Dutch/Danes/English	1630
Accra (Ft. James)	English	1673
Accra (Ussher)	Dutch	1649
Cape Coast (Ft. Victoria)	British	1702
Keta (Ft. Prinzenstein)	Danes	1784
Sekondi (Ft. Orange)	Dutch	1690
Dixcove (Metal cross)	English	1693
Teshie (Fort Augustaborg)	Danes	1787
Ada (Fort Kongenstein)	Danes	1783
Princestown (Fredrichsburg)	Brandenburgers	1683

Elmina

- Original name is 'Anum a ansa', meaning 'the well never dries'.

- Became known as 'Edina' which is a corruption of a Portuguese word 'Aldea' which means 'village'. Edina has erroneously become the indigenous name.

- Elmina, as the town is known today, is a corruption of Portuguese El mina meaning 'the mine'. The Portuguese upon their first contact with the community described it as a gold mine.

- Castle was built in 1482 and named Sao Georges (St. George's) after the patron saint of Portugal.

- The first church in the Gold Coast was built at Elmina at where Fort St Jago now stands, but later relocated to the Castle. The St. Joseph Church on top of the Kokodo hill remains the oldest Catholic Church in Ghana.

- A 'regimento agreement' in 1529 barred the locals from trading with other Europeans other than the Portuguese. Penalty was whipping and or chopping off an ear. The harshness and unfair treatment made the locals connive with the Dutch in 1637 to attack the Castle. The locals helped carry canons to the top of Ft. St. Jago Hill from where the attack was launched. The Dutch defeated the Portuguese on 29th August 1637 after two previous attempts.

- The town, like some others of similar experience, still exhibits some elements of European heritage as reflected not only in family names such as Bartels,

Ulzen, Van-Dyke, etc. but also in local festivals such as the Edina Bronya. Another aspect of shared European heritage is the taste for European items particularly Dutch (Java) wax print popularised by returnee Gold Coast soldiers who fought in the Dutch colonial army in (then) Netherlands East Indies. The Java Museum in Elmina best expresses this legacy.

- The British used the Elmina Castle as training grounds for English West African soldiers (comprising Gold Coast, Nigeria, Gambia, Sierra Leone) to prepare for the 2nd World War and were then sent to Burma (India) as Royal West African Frontier Force

- From 1948 till Independence, the Castle was used as Police training school.

Christiansborg (Osu)

- First started as a lodge by the Swedish African Company

- Captured by the Danes in 1657 who subsequently took over all Swedish property in the Gold Coast.

Cape Coast (Carbo Corso)

- Castle first started as a trading lodge in 1555 by the Portuguese who named the settlement 'Carbo Corso' meaning a short cape

- The Swedes built a permanent fort in 1653 and named it Fort Carolusburg, after King Charles X of Sweden

- Carolusburg changed ownership following its capture by the Danes, then by a local Fetu Chief before the Dutch captured it, all in the span of 11 years,

- Captured eventually by the English who held it till 1957,

the Castle became the seat of colonial Gold Coast government till 1877.

PEOPLING OF GHANA

West Africa before 1600

- Many kingdoms and empires arose in West Africa particularly in the Sudan area of savannah grassland between 1000 and 1600AD,

- Reasons

    » proximity of Sudan to the Sahara and trade routes across northern Africa which had numerous trade routes running south to the gold and salt producing areas of southern grassland and forests

    » development of agriculture using iron tools from as far back as 400 BC helped in the growth of population and urban settlement

    » creation of powerful armies using iron weapons

- Major empires within the period were **Ghana** (400-1240 AD), **Mali** (1240 -1500 AD) and Songhai(1460-1600 AD)

- Several new states subsequently emerged in West Africa due to the following reasons:

    » collapse/decline of the Sudanese empires and their replacement by new kingdoms,

    » continued growth of trade between Sudan and Guinea (zone)

    » the increase in central trade with Europeans especially with the expansion of the Atlantic Slave trade after 1650

- Movement of people into present-day Ghana is

characterized into 4 main groups namely the **Akan, Mole-Dagbani, Ga-Adangbe,** and the **Ewe.**

Mole-Dagbani

Ethnic groups include Gonja, Mamprusi, Dagomba, Nanumba, Konkomba, Wala, Sisala, Kasena-Nankana, Talensi, amongst others.

i. Gonja

- Migrated from Mande in present-day Senegal towards the end of the 16th Century

- Were led by Ndewura Jakpa,

- Met the Guan/Akan and subdued them and fought other groups such as the Dagomba to extend their kingdom

- Located in the SavannahRegion from Bole to Salaga with the traditional capital as Yaabon. Other towns include Damongo, Savelugu, Yapei and Buipe.

ii. Mamprusi

- Tohazie (the Red Hunter) led his group of warriors from near Lake Chad area in the 12th Century

- First settled at Pusiga and consolidated their control of the territory. Tohazie's grandson Bawa (or Gbewa)set up the Mamprusi kingdom

- His military and political prowess helped him to expand his territory

- Mamprusi is currently located in Upper East and North-East regions with important towns being Nalerigu,

Walewale, Pusiga, Gambaga and Bawku.

Dagomba

- Founded by Sitibo, Bawa's son

- His successor annexed several territories in late 15th Century and thus expanded the kingdom

- They were credited with technological prowess (e.g. 5-storey building, large underground water cistern, etc.)

- Became a tributary state of the Asante until 1874 when they were liberated following the signing of the Treaty of Fomena

Akan

- Believed to have migrated from ancient Sudanese empire (i.e. Ghana Empire)

- Originally known as the *Nta*-fo (group of Guan, Fante & Twi), they settled in the savannah-land of now western Gonja for many years

  » Guans: First to move southwards, down along river Volta and settled at the Afram Plains, then through Akwapim and further south to the coastal plains near Cape Coast. Scattered across today's Ghana and include Efutu/Awutu (CR), Larteh and Anum (ER), Nchumuru (Krachi), Nkonya, Likpe, Akpafu (OtiR).

  » Fante: Moved and settled at Takyiman (Techiman) and later moved southwards along the Tano river till they settled to the east of Cape Three Points. The Fante now occupy about half of the central region of Ghana.

» Twi: Last of the Nta-fo group to move from the north slowly southwards. Occupy present-day Asante, Akyem, Juaben, Kwahu and Akwamu. The Akwamu were the first Twi group to move southwards, settling at Nyanao hill near Nsawam. They expanded into a powerful kingdom in the 17th and 18th Centuries. The Akwamu are currently located around Akosombo-Atimpoku area.

» Asante: Largest of the Twi group, settled at Takyiman, Bono and Gyaman before moving to current location through Asantemanso and spread over current location. Bekwai, Kokofu, Kwaman, Mampong, Ejisu, Nsuta, Agogo, Obuasi are some of the Asante towns.

Ga-Adangbe

- Migrated from present-day Nigeria

- Some are said to have arrived by land, others by sea

- Present name *Ga* or *Nkran* in Akan (meaning *driver ants*) is in reference to the large numbers by which they arrived. They are believed to have arrived in early 15th Century.

- First lived inland in scattered communities, developing Ayawaso as their principal town. They regularly met at **Kpehe** (meeting place or market) to exchange their crops for fish.

- Moved to settle on the coast by early 17th Century in order to benefit from trade with the Europeans. Ga Mashi, Nungua and Tema moved to the coast first and were later followed by La and Osu. A dispute led to a section of the La people establishing a new settlement called Teshi.

- Each Ga settlement is made up of seven quarters (*akutsei*), subdivided into **we**. Each of the seven quarters of Ga had its own chief though, traditionally, they were ruled by priests (*Wulomei*)

- The seven quarters of Ga settlement are Asere, Abola, Gbese, Sempe, Akumadze, Otublohun and Alata

- Ga-Adangbe towns include Accra, Ada, Ningo, Prampram, Somanya, Agotime-Kpetoe (VR), Osudoku, Kpone and Dodowa

Ewe

- They trace their origin from Egypt through Sudan, Ethiopia, Yurobaland (Ile Ife in present-day Nigeria), Tado and Notsie, Togo

- Occupied Notsie for many decades under several good kings except one, King Agorkorli

- Rebelled and escaped from the brutal and cruel rule of King Agorkorli

- Moved out of Notsie in different groups such as the Gbi (comprising Peki and Hohoe), Anlo, Asorgli (Ho and neighborhood), Akpini (Kpandu), Ave (Dakpa) etc. Each group had its leader, which explains the several *paramountcies* found among the Ewe today.

- Settled by the eastern border of the Volta River from the coast to central Volta and inhabit the Volta Region today together with some Guan and Dangbe communities.

- A large part of it (apart from Anlo and Peki) had been under German administration (**German Togoland**) following the Berlin Conference in 1884-5, until the end of the 1st World War.

Population distribution of major ethnic groups (based on 2000 census)

Ethnic Group	Population distribution (%)
Akan	49.1
Mole Dagbani	16.5
Ewe	12.7
Ga -Adangbe	8.0
Guan	4.4
Gurma	3.9
Others	5.4

Note: There are about 67 ethnic and sub-ethnic groups in Ghana.

GHANA'S TOURIST ATTRACTIONS

Bono, Ahafo and Bono-East Regions

Land size: **39,557 km²**

Approximately 403 km from Accra to Sunyani.

- Duasidan Monkey Sanctuary, near Dormaa
- Buabeng-Fiema Monkey Sanctuary
- Buoyem Bat Caves
- Tanoboase Sacred Grove
- Kristoboase Catholic Monastery
- Kunsu Slave Camp, near Kintampo
- Fuller falls and Kintampo falls
- Bui Dam and City (Project)
- Bui National Park and Hippo Sanctuary
- Digya National Park
- Goitre Curing Spring at New Senya
- Kwaku Fri Shrine at Nwoase
- Hani Archaeological Site
- Nchiraa Falls
- Atebubu Bee Shrine
- Craft works: Kente weaving at Yamfo, Woodcarving at Odumase and Chiraa, Pottery at Adantia, Adinkra at Asuoye

Northern, North-East and Savannah Regions

Land size: **70,384 km²**
Approximately 654 km from Accra to Tamale

- Mole National Park (Wildlife and Slave History)

- Mognori Cultural Village

- Larabanga Ancient Mosque and Mystery Stone

- Nalerigu Defense Wall

- Gambaga Witches Camp and Nakpanduri Scarp, Witches Camps at Kukuo, Gnani, Gushegu, Kpatinga

- Karimenga Greenhouse and Eco-Village

- Daboya Cultural Village (Textiles, Fugu, Salt-Mines, Festival)

- Yendi (German War-Field, And Cemetery, Ancient Historical Monuments, *Jatropher* Plantation, Babatu's Grave)

- Sognon Traditional Buildings and Shrine, And Festival

- Kulmasa Crocodiles Pond

- Tamale Metropolis (Craft)

- Busunu and Jetile Slave History

- Salaga Former Slave Market and Slave Wells

- Buipe (Clinker Deposit and Cement Factory, BOST, Volta Lake, Yakambo Forest Reserve)

- Limestone Quarry at Buipe

- Yeji VLTC Ferry Crossing

- Damba Festival (Various Communities in August)

- Bugum Festival (Walawale)

- Xylophones at Glisiya (Near Bimbila)

Upper West Region

Land size: **18,476 km²**
721km from Accra to Wa

- Wechiau Hippo Sanctuary (Hippos, Cruising on Black Volta, Bird Watching, Lobi Culture)

- Balawa Bone Setting Centre (at Wa-West District)

- Gbelle National Park (Wildlife)

- Gwollu (Slave Defense Wall, Bone Treatment Center)

- Wuling Mushroom-shaped Rocks and Unique Landscape

- Kaleo and Sankana (Crocodile Pond, Slave Caves)

- Nandom/Lawra (Xylophones, Historical Prison where Nkrumah was imprisoned)

- Nakore Ancient Islamic Mosque and Heritage

- Bulenga Slave Caves

- Hamille And Dahili Caves (For Hiking)

- Wa (Metropolis, Colonial Cemetery, Wa Naa's Palace)

- Shrines (at Brifo Baa, Kyelee And Kala)

- Sacred Groves (at Tizza, Wagu, Legiri, Gyengyeng)

Upper East Region

Land size: **8,842 km²**
815km from Accra to Bolgatanga

- Paga Crocodile Ponds

- Tongo/Bongo Whistling Rocks and Landscape

- Sirigu Art Village (Paintings, Pottery and Local Women Entrepreneurship)

- Mother of Mercy Babies (Orphanage) at Sirigu

- Nania Slave Camp

- Naa Gbewaa's Shrine and Palace at Pusiga

- Bolgatanga Craft Center and Museum

- Widnaba Cultural Village and Landscape

- Navrongo (Mud Cathedral, Minor Basilica, War Memorial Hospital, Health Research Center, Tomb of Bagao – the notorious Slave-raider)

- Horseback Riding at Zokor And Bongo

- Yarigungu Crocodile Pond in Bawku

- Bawku Leather Tanning

- Kulungugu Memorial Grounds

- Fiisa Shrine in Sandema

- Fiok Festival (Sandema in November/December)

- Samampiid Festival in Bawku

- Gologo Festival at Tongo in March

Ashanti Region

Land size: **24,389 km²**

272km from Accra to Kumasi

- Lake Bosumtwi

- Kumasi (Manhyia Palace museum, Cultural Center, Okomfo Anokye Sword Site, Kejetia Open Market, Military Museum)

- Bonwire/ Ntonsu/Adanwomase Craft Villages

- Ejisu Besease Shrine

- Bobiri Butterfly Sanctuary (at Kubease)

- Owabi Bird Sanctuary

- Rattary Park

- Obuasi Goldmines

- Bomfobiri Wildlife Sanctuary

- Akwasidae Festival and Adae-Kese Festival

- Kwame Nkrumah University of Science and Technology (KNUST)

- Traditional Shrines at Adako Jachi, Patakro and Kentikronu

Eastern Region

Land size: **19,323 km²**
87km from Accra to Koforidua

- Waterfalls: Boti, Akaa, Asenema, Osuben, Begoro
- Scenic Views: Kwahu Hills, Akwapim Ridge
- Cocoa Research Institute of Ghana (CRIG) And Model Cocoa Farm
- Adjeikrom Cocoa Village (near Begoro)
- Obo Paragliding and Zipline Adventure
- CSRIPM now Centre for Plant Medicine Research
- Tetteh Quarshie Cocoa Farm at Mampong
- Akosombo Dam
- Bunso Aboretum and Canopy Walkway
- Klowem (Krobo) Mountains
- Abonse (Old) Slave Market
- Aburi Botanic Gardens
- Peduase Valley Resort
- Basel Mission Buildings at Akropong
- Okomfo Anokye Relics at Awukugua
- Traditional Shrines (Akonedi Shrine at Larteh, And Bruku at Kwahu Tafo)
- Crafts: Beads Industry and Market in Kroboland
- Koforidua Beads Market (Saturday/Thursday)
- Pottery Works in Kwahu areas
- Wood Carving at Aburi, Ahwerese, Nkawkaw, Enyiresi
- Odwira Festival (Akwapim, September/October)

- Dipo Festival (Krobo, March)
- Nmayem Festival (Manya Krobo, October)
- Kloyosikplemi Festival (Yilo Krobo, November)
- Ohum Festival (Akyem, June)
- Paragliding Festival at Kwahu At Easter (March/April)

Volta and Oti Regions

Land size: **20,570 km²**

Approximately 166km from Accra to Ho

- Wli Waterfalls and Agumatsa Wildlife Sanctuary (near Hohoe)

- Afadjato (At Liati Wote/Gbledi)

- Tagbo Waterfalls at Liati

- Tafi Monkey Sanctuary and Cultural Village

- Gemi Mountains and Amedzofe Scenic Village

- Ancestral Caves at Likpe and Kortini Mountain Resort (near Hohoe)

- Kyabobo National Park (at Nkwanta)

- Xavi Bird Sanctuary (near Akatsi)

- Shiare Terrace and Cultural Village

- Holy Trinity Spa and Farm (Sogakope)

- Keta Lagoon Complex and the Sea Defence Wall

- Limestone Caves at Logba Tota and Nyagbo Sroe

- German Historical Buildings at Kpandu, Kpeve, Ho, Amedzofe, Agove

- Bremen Village at Akoefe (near Ho)

- Catholic Grottos at Kpandu (Agbenoxoe and Aziavi)

- Shrines and Yewe Cult at Klikor, Nogokpo, Dzodze,

- Avakpe Rock and Cave at Kpodzivi (near Akatsi)

- Ave Dakpa Crocodile Pond

- Granite Rocks and Shrine at Akporkplor (near Xevi) (Shrine dislikes black costumes)

- Atorkorold Slave Market

- Keta Lagoon

- Craft: Iron Works at Akpafu, Alavanyo, Aveme

- Craft: Pottery Industry at Vume, Adutor, Lolito

- Craft: Kente Weaving at Kpetoe, Agbozume

- Kamor (Rice) Festival in Akpafu/ Santrokofi (January), Avatime (February)

- Agbamevorza (Kente Festival) in Kpetoe (August/ September)

- Pottery wok in Shai- Osudoku areas

- Hogbetsotso In Anlo In November

- Lekoryi Festival at Likpe (biennial, in March/April, during Easter)

- Agadevi Festival at Have

- Okyonsa Festival at Santrokofi

Greater Accra Region

Land size: **3,245 km²**

- Kwame Nkrumah Memorial Park
- Shai Hills Resource Reserve and Archaeological Site
- National Museum
- Fredriskgave Plantation & Slavery Lodge and Common Heritage Museum (at Sesemi, near Abokobi)
- W. E. B. Dubois Center
- George Padmore Research Library
- Accra Metropolis
- Old Accra and Brazil House
- Ghana Memorial Photo Gallery
- Herbal Market (Juju Market) at Arena
- Tema (Cocoa Processing Company, Harbour, etc.)
- Accra Mall
- Dodowa Forest and Chenku Falls
- University of Ghana
- Artists Alliance and Various Art Galleries
- Pottery Works in Okwenya/Shai Areas
- Songhor Lagoon and Salt Industry at Ada
- Homowo and Charle-Wote Festivals (Accra, August-September)
- Asafotufiam Festival (Ada – July/August)
- Schools Reunion Festival (September/October)

Central Region

Land size: **9, 826 km²**
145km from Accra to Cape Coast

- Elmina Castle and Historic Elmina Township

- Cape Coast Castle and Municipality

- Kakum National Park (Flora and Bird-Watching)

- Beach Resorts and Raw Beaches at Gomoa Fetteh, Coconut Grove, Brenu, Winneba, Biriwa

- Ramsar Site at Winneba

- Ceramics in Winneba

- Craft in Ajumako, Aboafu, Bobikuma, Otsew Jukwa, Assin Fosu

- Shrines (Posuban) at Elmina, Winneba, Mankesim, Apam

- Aboakyir Festival (in Winneba, May)

- Bakatue Festival (in Elmina, July)

- Fetu Afahye Festival in Cape Coast (September)

- PANAFEST/Emancipation (July/August)

- Masquerades Performances in Winneba, Elmina

Western and Western-North Regions

Land size: **23,921 km²**
Approximately 229 km from Accra to Takoradi

- Nzulezo Village-on-stilts

- Ankasa National Park

- Maritime Islands of Busua and Axim

- Beaches (Busua, Dixcove, Miamia, Axim, Beyin)

- Colonial Forts (Beyin, Sekondi, Axim, Dixcove, Butri, Shama, Princesstown)

- Nkroful (Nkrumah's hometown)

- Mines (Tarkwa, Prestea, Nsuta Awaso)

- Plantations: Rubber (GREL), Palm and Other Plantations

- Oil and Port City of Takoradi

- Kundum festival (Nzema, in October)

TRADITIONAL FESTIVALS OF GHANA

Introduction

Centuries-old traditions and culture remain a rich legacy for modern Ghana and has been an important tourism product for Ghana. Standing out are our traditional festivals which constitute significant elements in our traditional calendar. It is interesting to note that throughout the year, from January to December, there is one traditional festival or another being celebrated in some part of the country.

A. Role of Festivals in Ghana's Tourism

Recall the types of tourism being promoted in Ghana, i.e. **Heritage, Eco-tourism, Cultural tourism,** and **Conference tourism.**

Remember that Culture is a way of life that projects the identity of a people. Festivals, which constitute an aspect of culture, encourage people-centered tourism. The tour guide must therefore help the tourist to have a good appreciation of and thus enjoy the festivals.

B. What Constitute Ghanaian Traditional Festivals?

Ghanaian traditional festivals:
- are a day/period in our life during which we mark or remember some event/happening/situation

- usually involves a celebration and therefore festivities may form an important component

- could be to mark a happy event or remember a sad occurrence

- may be to venerate or give thanks to a supreme or supernatural being

- are generally **communal** events albeit some may be **group** or **personal** event

Examples:

- Personal festival: birthday, promotion, etc.

- Community or entire ethnic groups e.g. marking of migration

- Personal and communal: rites of passage e.g. puberty, marriage, funerals, naming and out-dooring ceremonies

C. Importance of Traditional Festivals

- They are occasions to celebrate/rejoice/make merry

- They promote social cohesion and friendship

- Revitalization of individual and communal spirit

- Education for the young vis-à-vis community customs, norms and traditions

- Constitute an instrument for propelling community development

- Respect, recognition and/or thanks-offering to ancestors and deities, etc.

- May mark the beginning or end of the traditional year

- Occasion to settle disputes among family/community members

D. Types of Traditional Festivals

Agricultural-Related Festivals

(i) To mark the beginning of an agricultural or a planting period/season e.g. Bakatue

(ii) To mark the beginning of a harvesting of a staple e.g. Teduza/Ngmayem/Homowo

(iii) To mark the end of the farming season e. g. Kamor festival

Religious Festivals

(i) **Veneration:** purely religious i.e. sacrifice to a supreme being e.g. Aboakyir

(ii) **Purification** e.g. Akwasidae, Adae (based on counting calendar), Ohum

Historical Festivals

To remember or re-enact a past event/situation/a calamity, e.g. Agadevi by Have community, Hogbetsotso by Anlo.

Social Festivals

Eg. Lekoryi of the Likpe people

Socio-Economic Festivals

E.g. PANAFEST

D. Major Elements/Components of the Traditional Festivals

a) Pre-festival/ preparation period

- Normally, takes a period of 2-8 weeks depending on festival

- To prepare for the festival

- Often times, involves a ban on one or other kind of activity e.g. excessive noisemaking

- Preparation is reminiscent of Lent/Advent in Christianity e. g. Homowo which places 6 weeks (40 days) ban on excessive noisemaking during which period millet for the ritual *kpoikpoi* is cultivated

- Period is used for executing private spiritual activities/ rituals by the elders, priests and chiefs on behalf of the people

- Period is used for confirming arrangements for logistics such as food, festival grounds, tents, drinks, invitees

b) Festival Period

- Can range from one day to 2 weeks

- The climax is usually a durbar which comes towards the end of the festival

- Durbar showcases the material and non-material culture of the community

- Ingredients include music, dances, drums, language, hierarchy among chiefs, paraphernalia, folklore, etc.

c) Post-festival period

Period used for evaluation and assessment.

- Clearing of environmental mess

- Stock taking (what went well and what went wrong and how to avoid it in the future)

- Was the development objective met?

- Financial accounts: bills to be paid, debts, how are they to be cleared, etc.

- Any cultural norms violated? How to deal with culprits, etc.

F. Unique Elements in Ghanaian Traditional Festivals

The following constitute special elements that stand out either in part or wholly, during the celebration.

- Special foods and drinks are provided either to fulfil the spiritual needs, or to enhance the merriment in some of the celebration. Some of these foods are especially reserved for the celebration and have, thus, become synonymous to the festival. Examples include *ortor* and eggs, *kpoikpoi*, *kodzan*, *gmedan*, *aliha* and palm-wine.

- Special dresses e.g. raffia-skirts, jute dresses, masks, leaves, beads, special hairstyle, amulets, tatters, etc.

- Special games e.g. *ekpo*, archery, *pilolo*, *pinpinaa*, wrestling, *ampe*, *ngblelo*

- Special dances e.g. *kundum*, *obese*, *atsiagbekor*, *kete*, *baya*, *takai*

- Open condemnation or praise e.g. *kpanshimo*, *ayodede*, *kpledjo*

A. Festival Types

i) Historical festival

Town/community	Region	Date/Period
Nkyidwo, Essumeja	Ashanti	June
Agadevi, Have	Volta	June
Bugum/Tamale/Wa/Lar abanga	Upper West/Northern	Usually after Hajj
Asafotufiam, Ada	Greater Accra	August (1st weekend)
Odambea, Akyemfo (Saltpond)	Central	August (Last Saturday)
Dayibakaka Akpini (Kpandu)	Volta	August
Sometutuzan, Some	Volta	August/September
Sasabobrim, Awuah-Domase	Central	November
Hogbetsotso, Anlo	Volta	Nov. (1st weekend)
Fiok, Builsa (Sandema)	Upper East Region	December
Glidzi, Adaklu	Volta	July

Kpalikpakpazan, all Kpalime communities	Volta	December (1st Week)
Lukusi, Ve	Volta	Novemer
Ntoafo Kuo Kese, Nkoranza	Bono- East	January

ii) Agric (Planting/Harvest)

Town/community	Region	Date/Period
Gologo, Talensi	Upper East	March
Ngmayem, Odumase	Eastern	October
Damba, Gonja, Mamprusi, etc.	Northern/Volta/Upper East/Upper West	August
Bakatue, Elmina	Central	July (1st weekend)
Homowo, Ga (Accra)	Greater. Accra	August - Sept
Kundum, Ahanta, Nzema	Western	August – Nov.
Kobine, Lawra	Upper West	November
Amu (Rice), Amedzofe	Volta	November
Kpini (Guinea fowl), Dagomba, Chokosi, Gonja	Norther, Savannah	December

iii) Religious: Veneration/Purification

Town/community	Region	Date/Period
Kwafie, Dorma-Ahenkro	Berekum AhafoDec	January
Edina-Bronya, Elmina	Central	January (1st Thursday)
Kpledjo, Tema	Greater Accra	March/April
Aboakyir, Simpa (Winneba)	Central	May (1st weekend)
Fetu Afahye, Oguaa (Cape Coast)	Central	September (1st wk)
Odwira, Akuapem	Eastern	Sept/October
Odwira, Jachie	Ashanti	January
Akwasidae, Asante, Manhyia	Ashanti	Every 40 days
Kloyosiklpemi, Yilo (Somanya)	Eastern	November
Apoo, Techiman	Bono-East	November

iv) Social/Socio-Cultural

Town/community	Region	Date/Period
Lekoryi, Likpe	Oti	Easter Saturday ((biennial)
Dipo Yilo & Manya Krobo	Eastern	April/ May
Otsobisa, Santrokofi	Oti	June
Afenorto, Mepe	Volta	July/August
Kusakorkor, Vane (Amedzofe)	Volta	December

v) Socio-Historical

Town/community	Region	Date/Period
Sasadu/Alavanyo/Sovie/Saviefe	Volta	October/November
Agumatsa, Wli	Volta	October
Gbidukorzan, Gbi (Hohoe)/Peki	Volta	December
Golofose, Alavanyo	Volta	November

vi) Socio-Political

Town/community	Region	Date/Period
Emancipation – Ghana/African Diaspora	Greater Accra, Central	August
PANAFEST – Ghana/African Union/International Community	Central, Greater Accra	July (biennial)

ACCRA

- Christiansborg Castle at Osu was once taken over and controlled by Nana Asamani, a trader from Akwamu in the 17th Century. Using trickery, he entered the Castle in the company of about a dozen other men purporting to buy firearms. Unknowing to the Danish officers, the buyers carried bullets, which they had hidden under their cloths. As soon as they were able to outsmart the colonial folks, they captured everyone and took control over the Castle. Asamani made himself Governor for about a year before negotiating to hand back the castle. (More details in the book Romancing Ghanaland by Kofi Akpabli).

- The Ga people are said to have arrived in their current location in early 15th Century. They met some Guan settlers in the area which was rich in anthills. The rather large number in which they arrived made the Guan who first saw them to describe them as having descended like ants which is nkran in Akan or gaga in Ga. This got corrupted to 'Accra' or 'Ga' as the case may be.

- Traditionally, Ga-Mashie comprised seven quarters namely Abola, Asere, Gbese, Otublohun (which collectively is known as Bukomor Kinka), and Sempe, Akumadze, and Alata collectively referred to as Ngleshie or Jamestown.

- The symbol of the Ga Paramountcy is an elephant with a duiker on top to signify that, though a small community, they can conquer nations.

- In the wake of European arrival, Bukom and Jamestown

unofficially became organised into two respective clusters/settlements of **Dutch Accra** and **British Accra**, respectively. These Europeans forged alliances with some of the Chiefs within their enclaves. These relationships trickled down to the rest of the people under the Chiefs, to the point that it resulted in rivalry and petty wars among the locals. The third cluster is **Danish Accra** around Osu.

- With the establishment of the first elementary school in Accra, Sempe Boys Government School, and later Accra Academy among others, Jamestown became an elite town comprising lawyers, doctors and business men. The first Gold Coast (Ghanaian) Barrister-at-Law in the person of Mr. Edmund Bannerman was from Jamestown. The Dutch Accra cluster of Kinka was a bit late in having access to formal education.

- Much of the architecture and buildings in Accra reflect the historical periods and sentiments e. g. Anglo-Indian (Wato Club), British countryside (Railway station) and imperial Britain (General Post Office completed in 1940).The defunct Sea View Hotel, the first hotel in Accra, was built around the time of the *Sagrenti* War between the Asante and the British. British journalists who covered the war in 1873 – 74 lodged in the Sea View hotel. .

- One prominent building is the Wesley (Methodist) Cathedral which took 40 years to build, from 1920 to 1960. Methodism and Anglicanism gained ground in the community thanks to the presence of the English. The St. Mary's Anglican Church was built to cater for the many locals who were not literate in English at the time and could thus not worship conveniently in the

Holy Trinity Cathedral (where English was the language of worship.

- Within the Osu area also emerged the Basel Mission quarters (Salem)

- Accra took over from Cape Coast as capital of Gold Coast in 1877, during the time of Tackie Tawiah I, legendary chief of Ga-Mashie. He ruled for 40 years (1862–1902) and was exiled several times by the British Administration to Elmina Castle for his opposition to colonialism. He fought resolutely to preserve and promote the good elements of Ga culture while abolishing obnoxious customs such as human sacrifice. He was also instrumental in making Accra the center of political, commercial and diplomatic activities. The title of **'King'** was first conferred on him (and 2 others – Asantehene and King Ghartey of Simpa) by the British for great leadership.

- **Victoriaborg** marked the beginning of residential diversification of Accra (1890s). Hitherto, both the Europeans and indigenes were living together at Ga-Mashie, but health insecurity compelled the Europeans to relocate to the segregated settlement of Victoriaborg, now called **Ridge**.

- Boundary Road (re-named Kojo Thompson Road in the 1980s) marked the boundary between local settlement and the new European quarters for white merchants and white Civil Servants. Africans were not allowed access to Victoriaborg after 6 p.m.

- The 6.00pm. ban was because the Europeans were of the view that the mosquitoes and other disease-carrying insects were more active from 6.00pm. till daybreak. Between the two townships of Adabraka and Victoriaborg was a fallow portion of land as buffer zone against mosquitoes and other insects. This is because the Europeans believed also that air and sunshine could keep away the mosquitoes. Hence, the typical stilts buildings at Ridge to raise the buildings high up in order to get enough air. The numerous windows per building are also to keep the insects at bay. Additionally, the *neem* tree was introduced to the European area of residence because the tree is known to produce a sap that repels insects. Recall that communities such as Cantonments, Labone, Ringway Estates and Kanda (all areas for the privileged then) had trees planted in front of the houses and along the avenues. Houses in these areas are also set some meters away from the street unlike you'll find in indigenous Ga areas such as Jamestown, Korle-Gonno, Chorkor, etc. and where the roads have therefore become an extension of their private compounds. It is therefore not uncommon, till date, to see roads blocked off at any time for social and private functions especially from Thursdays to Sundays.

- The fallow track of land (between Adabraka and Victoriaborg) was utilised after Independence for state buildings including the National Museum, State Hotels Corporation, Accra Workers' College and Accra Polytechnic among others.

- The European Hospital (later Ridge and now Gt. Accra Regional Hospital) was established to take care exclusively of European expatriates at the time.

- **Adabraka** was the next township to develop as a result of Accra residential diversification program. Following the yellow fever outbreak in Ga-Mashie in 1911, middle-class Ga, including servants of colonial officers, took hire-purchase loans to build the 1st African middle-class settlement in Accra under the name Adabraka.

- This opened the way for other new settlements in response to natural disasters or for commercial expediency. For example, **Kaneshie** with its low-cost houses emerged in late 1930s as government-planned township following the earthquake that destroyed several houses in then Accra. The new settlement was dominated by non-indigenous Ga (mainly Akan).

- **Korle-Gonno** had already started as a quarantine point for the 1908 bubonic plague victims. Most of these victims were from the Alata group and had been quarantined for a long time. Hence, upon a request from their chief after the plague, houses were provided for them by the government, turning it into a new Ga settlement. Note that the bubonic plague was what compelled the British to relocate the seat of Government to the Christiansborg Castle.

- Asylum Down was a farmland with water-wells that was settled by returnee slaves from Brazil to practice their 'modern' farming skills acquired from Brazil, other returnee professionals who settled at Asylum Down and surrounding areas of Kokomlemle include tailors like the Mortons. This explains why the Tabon Street and Nassau Street in Asylum Down.

- **Makola** was occupied by Yoruba cattle merchants from 'Omokolade' in early 1900s, they used to line up their cows for sale along the Cowlane. Nima; later developed following a hike in fees charged for cows at Makola (Cowlane). They moved the market to Nima as an alternative in the 1940s.

- The fire that engulfed Makola in 1916 saw a lot of Yuroba merchants move to Tudu, where it became a great commercial enclave housing shops like Kingsway, cloth sellers, etc. The Tudu lorry station was therefore built by the British in 1928 and served as commercial point for potters from the northern Ghana and who settled at Sabon Zongo. Makola No. 1 was rebuilt in 1924 following the fire outbreak.

- Demobilised soldiers who had fought in the British-Asante wars were also resettled at Tudu from Salaga Market area. The fact is that most of these soldiers were Ibo and Hausa from Nigeria, because the British had at the time resorted to conscription of non-Christians into the army; because they were not only ready to take orders but were also strong and more physically fit. This was in contrast with their Christian counterparts who were known to complain too much. This very reason explains why, even for a long time after Independence, Ghana's Army was still dominated by the Moslems from northern Ghana because the new Administration simply carried on with the colonial British model.

- **Salaga Market** was an important trading point for the Asante who, by virtue of their controlling of Dagomba area, had a lot of war captives who they brought to Salaga market to sell. Recall that the Dutch and the Asante had a good business relationship, hence the situating of the market close to the Dutch trading fort. (Some other historians however are of the view that the market developed in 1874 as a deliberate onslaught against Asante control of the Kintampo trade route.) Some of the Nigerian soldiers who had fought in the

Sagrenti War were first settled in the Salaga market area which therefore became the first migrant community (which is commonly referred to as Zongo) in Ghana.

- The cenotaph inside Salaga market was built in 1901 in honor of the soldiers who died whilst fighting on the side of the British in the 1900 Yaa Asantewa war. The other cenotaph by the James Fort was erected to honour soldiers who fell in the Sagrenti War while fighting on the side of the British.

- The Ga had earlier on resisted European invasion into their community until one of their chiefs gave permission for the Dutch to build the Ussher Fort (built in 1649). This opened the way for the Swedes to build Christiansborg Castle and, later, James Fort by the English. The initial resistance of the locals (Ga) to colonial slavery is reflected in the traditional layout of old Accra. The rather clumsy layout is a deliberate plan to protect themselves against slave trade, hence the seeming disorder in their building layout which made it difficult for a stranger to get out once inside the compound or arena. The architecture and layout promoted the attitude of neighbourliness among the people and hence it is not unusual even today to hear one shout from one's house to the other house across the street as the street is not seen as a barrier in this case. In fact, it was this very safeguarding of themselves against slave trade that gave rise to the institution of chieftaincy amongst the Ga. Their desire for a strong military authority to deal with their perpetrators made them adopt the chieftaincy concept from the Akan (namely Akwamu, Akyem and Asante). This became necessary because the Wulomei, their traditional leaders, would not spill blood. Even today, many of Ga royal court ceremonies are performed using Akan e. g. drum language.

- In the wake of political struggle for Independence in 1940s and 1950s, three important venues for political activities emerged. The ground on which Usher Clinic now stands was used for UGCC political rallies while Arena and Palladium were popular rally grounds for CPP.

- **Achimota:** The place was inhabited by slaves and hence *names* were not required to be called there so as not to reveal the origin of the people. Recall that, apart from the transatlantic slave trade, local slave trade did take place even way beyond 1807 when the English had abolished the practice thanks to efforts of William Wilberforce and others. Local slaves were used as servants in homes, farms and as trade representatives for their masters while some were used for sacrifices.

- **Abavana Junction:** Located on the Pig Farm–Accra Newtown Road, Abavana Junction in Kotobabi was named after Mr. Lawrence R. Abavana of Navrongo in the Upper East Region. He was the first Commissioner of the Northern Territories (comprising the five regions of the north). He was also the first MP for his area and a Cabinet Minister in Nkrumah's government. This junction and neighborhood were named after him because he was one of the first residents to put up a house which still stands at the location. '*Abavana*' in Kasem language means "I don't deny a good request.". (More details in '*A Sense of Savannah – Tales of a Friendly Walk Through Northern Ghana*' by Kofi Akpabli).

- **Dodowa** was a major trading center in early 1900s when palm oil was the country's main export (to Europe) until cocoa replaced the industry in early 1930s. From the Akwapim ridge, casks of palm oil were rolled down to Dodowa. The town was also a major center for gold-smithing.

- Note however that the Ga-Adangbe, just like the Ewe, traditionally use beads rather than gold for adornment. Gold ornaments mainly serve as adornments for the Asante.

- Beads can be made in Ghana from different objects, namely seeds, bones, shells, rock, glass and plastics. Different types of beads are worn on different parts of the body, at different occasions, and for various reasons which may include:

  » Aesthetics/adornment (jewelry)

  » rank or position in society

  » victory/success/satisfaction

  » spiritual protection/ward off evil spirits

  » enhancement of physical beauty e. g. shaping the waist or other parts of the body

  » regulate bodyweight

  » sexual foreplay device/sexual relationship stimulant

  » luck/good fortune

  » give identity e. g. twins

THE UPPER REGIONS

- The Volta River and Volta Lake as they are known largely in southern Ghana, actually started out as three tributaries of the same river that has its source in Burkina Faso. The Red, White and Black Voltas then course through the Upper East, Upper West, Savannah and Northern Regions before joining together further south. Travelling from Accra towards Tamale, visitors encounter the BlackVolta at Buipe and the White Volta at Yapei. The Red Volta flows from the Bawku area of Upper East Region (more details in '*A Sense of Savannah – Tales of a Friendly Walk Through Northern Ghana*' by Kofi Akpabli).

- Ethnic groups include the Kassena, Nankani, Tallensi, Gurunsi, Builsa, Kusasi, Dagaaba, Sissala, Wala and Lobi.

- The area was subjected to exploits of notorious slave-raiders such as Samori, Babatu, and Bagao in mid 1800s to early 1900s, using camps like Nania and Mole, and ending up in Salaga market

- Area largely resorted to huts with flat roofs made of clay to **(i)** escape the frequent torching of the huts by the slave raiders, **(ii)** monitor the activities of the raiders from the roof top, **(iii)** dry crops (cereals, peanuts, etc.) and keep them out of reach of domestic animals (today, flat top spaces are used for these purposes), and **(iv)** for sleeping in the open due to the intense heat during the hot seasons

- Many of their buildings are circular in structure (round) to protect them against the wind as well as against the heat (refer to eddy current concept in Physics)

- Individual compounds are generally distance away from one another (200–400m), guaranteeing land for their subsistence farming around the compounds. Thus, settlements (villages) are generally dispersed over a large area.

- Area officially became part of the Gold Coast colony in 1901 as part of the Northern territories.

- Navrongo and North-Western part of UWR region are strongly rooted in Catholicism. Catholicism in Northern Ghana started from Navrongo in 1905 and later spread across the area. Jirapa was the first community in now Upper West Region to accept Christianity (Catholicism), laying the cornerstone for the church on December 12, 1929.

- The Credit Union scheme in Africa (and in Ghana for that matter) started from there – specifically in Jirapa – in 1955. The scheme was introduced by the Catholic church of Wa. By 2010 there were over 260 credit unions in Ghana with over 200,000 members that keep expanding and spreading among organised labour unions and church groups.

- First baptism for 12 successful catechumen in Upper West region included the late Cardinal Poku Dery (made a Cardinal in 2006). Wa became a Diocese in 1959. Ghana now has 19 Dioceses and 1 vicariate.

GWOLLU

- Chief Tanga around the 19th Century built a slave defense wall with peep-holes to protect the community from the exploits and harassment by notorious slave raiders like Samori. Inner and outer walls were built round the village and farmlands respectively. The inner wall took two years to complete; its remnant is now protected for tourism and for posterity. The town is also renowned for its bone-setting clinic. It also has the tomb of Dr. Hilla Limann who was the President of the Third Republic.

- Gwollu is the capital of Sissala West District

- Shea trees are dominant in Northern, Savannah, North-East and Upper West Regions. The scientific name is Butyrospermum Parkii, named after Mungo Park, the so-called discoverer of the tree in the 18th Century.

- The shea tree has the following uses:

  » Leaves are used for flavoring and decoration

  » Leaves served as garment for Lobi women in the past

  » Fruit is edible and many times sustains the people as snacks, especially when working in the field

  » Nut is processed into shea butter for local cuisine and cosmetic industry. Processing involves boiling of nuts, drying in the sun, pounding or milling, and boiling of the paste to get butter/oil.

  » Dead shea wood is used as keys of the xylophone, a popular musical instrument in northern Ghana.

NB: Shea trees mainly grow in the wild in Ghana but are now cultivated in Burkina Faso. The fruiting season is May–July, therefore picking of the nuts falls within this period. Women in northern Ghana are organising into cooperative groups in shea butter processing.

NAVRONGO

- *Na'voro* as original name, meaning *I have stepped on soft ground* in Kassen language (ref. Butu, the founder)

- **1904:** A garrison was opened by the British in Navrongo to stem the prevalent tribal conflicts and slave raiders activities

- **1905:** Bagao, a notorious slave raider in the area, was captured by British forces and executed having earlier on been tied to a stake allowing the locals to taunt him. (Remember that slave raids were officially stopped by the British and the French in 1897.)

- **1906:** Catholic missionaries (Morin, Chollet and Eugene) first arrived in Navrongo to start evangelizing the locals, the mud Cathedral (now mini-Basilica) was built in 1920

- **1918:**Spanish flu epidemic killed about 10,000 people in and around Navrongo

- **1920:** First bicycle appeared in Navrongo (recall that it's an area inundated by bicycles and motorcycles today as the main means of transport)

- **1927:** Telephone introduced in Navrongo for the first time

- **1935:** War Memorial Hospital was built as well as a number of schools. The hospital today is a research hospital for the Ministry of Health and it's here that kwashiorkor was first discovered

- **1940:** Paga airstrip was built in readiness for imminent German invasion from Ouagadougou

- Special wall decorations are a cultural peculiarity of the Sirigu – Navrongo area. Women take pride in enhancing the beauty of the houses of their husbands. They use local materials to paint on a flat surface or in relief. Using usually black, red and white colors, they come out with patterns full of symbolic meanings.

- Examples:

  Cattle: as symbol of wealth (and sometimes discipline and orderliness)

  Broken calabash: expression of ever useful and recycling

  Python: totem symbol of [clan] protection

  Male symbols: portray the masculinity of humans

  Female symbols: show feminine aspect of humans and animals

  Christian objects: referring to their strong Christian roots dating back from 1906, they normally combine these with traditional symbols to reflect a merger of two cultures.

NKRUMAH AND NKRUMAISM

- Kwame Nkrumah was born on 21 Sept 1909 at Nkroful in the Western Region of Ghana.

- Attended Half Assini R.C. Basic school, then continued at various stages to Achimota, a seminary; Lincoln College (in the USA where he spent 10 years), and the UK (where he spent 2 years)

- Returned to Gold Coast in Nov. 1947 to work for United Gold Coast Convention (UGCC)

- As a General Secretary, he was meeting with other leading party members at Saltpond in Canaan Lodge, a property of Mr. Albion Mends (the first postmaster of Gold Coast) who was the Treasurer of UGCC. Albion was a friend to J. B. Danquah. The party meetings later moved to Hammond Hall also in Saltpond. At Saltpond, Nkrumah was sleeping in the 33-steps House (Room No. B16)

- Nkrumah later broke away to inaugurate the Convention People's Party (CPP) on 12 June 1949 in Accra after earlier meetings at Tarkwa towards forming the new party. The breakaway was upon the encouragement of Kweku Baako Snr.

- Nkrumaism comprises 4 elements:

  » Social justice and equal opportunity for all

  » Self-determination

  » Self-reliance

  » Pan-Africanism (Pan-African movement)

- These elements find expression in the provision of

food, education, health, and social benefits. Simply, Nkrumaism culminates in 'building a nation' by bringing together all the facets of the nation

- Examples reflect in Housing Estates in Mamprobi, South Labadi, Ringway, etc. in the 1950s

- Nkrumah established 67 State enterprises such Black Star Line, Ghana Airways, Meat Factory, Shoe Factory.

- Creation of schools across the country including Workers' College. He also built health facilities across the country

- Introduced Workers' Brigade

- In short, everything was well-thought out to ensure the dignity of the Ghanaian on the basis of a welfare state namely, eradicating idleness, squalor, disease, ignorance and want.

- He established the Kwame Nkrumah Ideological Institute at Winneba which now houses the Southern Campus of the University of Education.

-

Centre for Plant Medicine Research – Mampong

- Established by Dr Oku Ampofo

- In the early 1960s, Dr Nkrumah sent Dr Ampofo and a team to China for further studies in herbal medicine

- In 1971, Dr Ampofo together with the Academy of Arts and Sciences and other interested organisations sent a proposal to the then government to take over and transform it into a Research Centre

- In 1975,the National Redemption Council (NRC) government through NRC Decree 344 accepted the proposal and transformed it into a scientific Research Centre Into Plant Medicine

- The Centre currently researches into plant medicine and cultivates herb farms in various ecological zones to sustain the industry

- It also carries out tests to determine efficacy and safety of herbal drugs by practitioners towards licensing by Food and Drugs Authority (FDA)

Ghana Crude Oil Industry

- Oil exploration started in Ghana since the 1890's, e.g. Saltpond Oil fields had produced oil in Ghana in small commercial quantity for a while, but shut down in 1970s

- GNPC was established in the 1980s to promote exploration activity in Ghana

- Current oil find (as at 2013) of about 300 million barrels, with prospects of up to 1.2 billion barrels in the Tano basin, with high concentration of gas

- Commercial drilling started on 15th December 2010 (NB: Commercial oil exploration leads to profit after all the interest and royalties have been paid)

- Current drilling is offshore

- Royalty approach being adopted in Ghana, hence investors come with their own machinery and funds (for the industry that is so capital intensive)

- Jubilee Fields has capacity to produce 120,000 barrels a day, but currently producing 100,000 barrels a day.

- The industry keeps expanding in terms of more finds and revenue

Ghana and Diamond

- 1st diamond export from Ghana was from Abomosu in 1919

- Diamond is mainly mined at Akwatia located in the Birim enclave

Christian Health Facilities in Ghana

- Christian groups play a major role in health delivery in Ghana

- Operates under the umbrella of Christian Health Association of Ghana (CHAG)

- CHAG as at 2016 provides about 40% of Ghana's health care. The Association comprises 21 Christian Church denominations, and has 291 Christian Hospitals, Clinics and Health Training Institutions with most of their facilities located in the remote areas within the country.

- CHAG pioneered the Health Insurance scheme in Ghana (at Nkoranza and Damongo) before it was adopted by the government as a nationwide scheme in early 2000.

Kente cloth

Normal male size: 14 strips, normal female size: 24 strips

Stools

3 types of stools:

i) ordinary stools

ii) ritual stools

iii) ceremonial stools

Stools embody a lot of symbols, e.g. **Ananse** – symbol of wisdom to denote for example a wise chief; **elephant** to denote highest authority, etc.

Mediums of Exchange and Currency Evolution in Ghana

- Barter system of exchange in early times

- Gold dust (esp. in Asante)

- Cowry shells (**sidie**) in pre-colonial period running into colonial times when it was used side-by-side with the pound and shilling

- Schnapps bottles

- 1916 - 1957: West Africa currency – West Africa pound, shillings and pence

- 1958 - 1965: Ghanaian Pound

- 1965 onwards: Cedis and pesewas

Some Slave Prices in the Gold Coast

In 1889, a German traveler to Salaga discovered the selling values for the following:

300 cowries for a female slave

400 cowries for a male slave

500 cowries for an ox

1000 cowries for a horse

150 cowries for a sheep

- Most of Ghana's Military Barracks bear names of 1st and 2nd World War battle towns e.g. Kamina Barracks, after (the town) Kamina in Togo. Kamina was a wireless station by the Germans then in Togo on the Lome-Atakpame road (about 4 hours' drive from Lome). The Germans were said to have destroyed the station using fuel, when the Allied Forces closed in on the Station. Other barracks include Burma (India), El-Wak, Gondar, etc.

- The Flagstaff house used to be the seat of the Commander of the West African Frontier Force until Nkrumah took it over.

- Vume – a Denkyira community now located in the Volta Region, migrated following war with the Asante. Name ye hume' corrupted to Vume. Very fine clay found in the area, some Kpandu potters come there for their clay

- Atorkor (near Whuti) – ator akor: a slave transit point and market

- Family cemeteries/mausoleums are common in Anlo land

- Individual wells are dug to water crops in Anlo land

Nsawam and Bread Industry in Ghana

- Once upon a time, Nsawam was synonymous with quality bread. All travelers along the Accra–Kumasi road made Nsawam a popular if not mandatory stop-over, just for its bread as a valuable gift to folks back home. That was in the mid-1950s to 1960s when Nsawam was a flourishing commercial town thanks to the booming cocoa industry around the Akwapim area.

- Nsawam became a bread centre, supplying travelers as well as both expatriate and local residents around Accra, Koforidua and the like. The woman at the centre of affairs was the late Mrs. Charlotte Longdon, who did not only rely on quality flour but also mobilised a lot of young ladies into a union of bakers. She was very popular for her unique oblong-shaped *Timber* bread. The quality of her bread and related confectionery products led to then Gold Coast Railway Authority granting her the license as sole vendor at Nsawam Railway station.

- In 1939, her Warabeba Industries won the contract (signed by Lord Swinton, Resident Representative of Allied Forces at Achimota) to solely supply the Allied Forces in West Africa, Burma and North Africa with food preserves including jams, biscuits, jellies, guava, etc. during the Second World War.

- Warabeba Industries which later metamorphosed into Warabeba IDC following government's involvement as a shareholder. It was sold out in 1967 by the NLC Administration.

The Akwapim Ridge

- The Akwapim Ridge is part of the Ghana-Togo ranges, with the Akwapim stretch lying close to Accra

- It has an average elevation of 450 m and has 22 close-set towns located on the Ridge, with Amanokrom at 500 m above sea level (a.s.l.) and 52 km from Accra. Other townships include Aburi (41 km and 457m a.s.l.), Mampong (50 km), Akropong (57 km), Larteh (60 km), Awukugua (58 km), with the State-owned Peduase Lodge (at Peduase, 35 km) which served as a residence for Ghana's President in the Second Republic.

- The Peduase Lodge also hosted in 1967, under the leadership of General Ankrah, the delegates to the Aburi Peace Accord (Peace talks) between General Odumegwu Ojukwu and Federal leadership of Nigeria to avert further bloodshed in the Biafran war of Nigeria.

- Akwapim Ridge gained the attention of Europe in 1788 thanks to the exploration of the area by Dr. Paul Isert, a Danish-born German botanist. Isert described the area as a 'Paradise' due to its cool weather, as opposed to the rather hot and humid weather in Accra. The altitude and absence of barrier on its seaward side accounts for the cool weather.

- In 1875, the British colonial Government built a health

resort at Aburi to serve as a convalescing centre for colonial officials. This was transformed into the first Agricultural Station in the Gold Coast in 1890, with the objective of finding suitable economic plants for European markets as well as experiment on suitability of economic and decorative plants from other tropical countries under Gold Coast's local conditions.

- The Agricultural research motive was abandoned in 1928 when it was converted into a botanical garden and opened to the public for recreational purposes since then. The Garden comprises 65 hectares, including 12 hectares yet to be developed

- The Garden used to house the 2nd oldest Post Office in the Gold Coast, as well as a Horticultural School which has now been revived.

- Lady Knustford tree, a silk cotton tree, remains the oldest, tallest and biggest tree in the Garden today as the sole survivor of the original forest. Lady Knustford was the wife of Lord Knustford, the British Secretary of State for the colonies in 1887–1892, the latter being instrumental in the establishment of the Garden.

- The Garden has themed lawns e.g. Spices Lawn, Children's Lawn, Royal Lawn, etc. and has tropical trees such as Monkey Pot tree from Brazil, Royal Palm from Cuba (planted in 1900) and four types of bamboo including the yellow-stem specie from China.

- In 1920, a motor car climbed Aburi hills for the first time, years after the first motor car arrived in the Gold Coast for the use of then Governor Nathan

- The Akwapim Ridge is strongly rooted in Presbyterianism,

boasting historical monuments such as Akropong College of Education (built in 1848 as the 2nd oldest tertiary Educational institution in West Africa), Larteh Basel Mission Church (1908), and European cemetery at Akropong

- Tetteh Quarshie cocoa farm is found at Mampong (cultivated in1879)

- As far back as 1871, the Bible was translated into the local language, Akwapim Twi, thanks to Christaller Akrofi who now has Akrofi–Christaller Theological Institute at Akropong named after him.

Shai/Kroboland

- Shai is an ethnic group now located in present Greater Accra Region

- The area has towns such as Dodowa and Agomeda

- The Shai people lived in caves within present Shai Hills Reserve as ancestral home until forced out by the British in late 1800s

- Area is rich in fine clay and hence is home to beautiful pottery and ceramics

- Shares boundary with the Krobo, Akwapim and Ga

- Krobo is an ethnic group belonging to the larger Dangbe group

- Comprises Yilo and Manya divisions

- Both divisions lived together (from mid 1700s) in their ancestral home on top of the Krobo (Klowem) mountain, an isolated hill on the Accra plains

- The group was forced out and relocated in present location by the British Colonial government under Governor William Griffith in 1892

- Ejected for reasons including, a) hiking of palm oil prices and refusal to sell to the British for 6 years in the 1800s, b) resistance to British Colonial rule

- They are very much known for a vibrant beads industry as well as the famous Dipo initiation rites into womanhood.

Child Naming and Names among Ghanaians

- The Ghanaian child is traditionally named on the 8th day of his/her birth. The reason is to be sure that the child has indeed come to stay "and not just passing by" as was the case of many changelings in the past. In fact, several rituals including specific names were employed for such changelings referred to in Ewe as dzikuidzikui. If a baby dies before the 8th day, traditionally it is treated as a mere visitor who has left his host and no serious funeral is observed. Hence, the new-born is required to survive the 7th day to be formally welcomed and accepted into the community.

- The number 7 is synonymous to perfection in the traditional Ghanaian setup. This concept of perfection is manifested in the chief's entourage of 7 horn-blowers as is common among some Guan/Akan communities whereby the King/Chief is heralded by 7 horn-blowers (sometimes 7 on either side) during official and court functions. This practice is clearly projected at Kwame Nkrumah Memorial Park in Accra.

- Between the day of birth and the official naming

ceremony, the child is addressed by his/her 'Day name', also known as Soul name. This set of names particularly common among Akan, Guan and Ewe groups have distinct names for male and females, although there may be some slight pronunciation nuances depending on which of these ethnic groups is involved. Soul names such as Adjoa, Abena, Akua, Yaa, Afia, Ama and Akosua. are used for girls whilst Kojo, Kwabena, Kwaku, Yaw, Kofi, Kwame and Kwesi are used for boys. (See Appendix for full detail)

- Child naming is performed in the morning to stress the beginning of life. In the very old days, the child was confined and restricted from outside contact except with the parents and very close trustworthy family members. This was so to keep the child from harm as belief in charms and evil spirit was rife then.

- At the ceremony, cold water is sprinkled on the child to introduce him/her to the realities and challenges of life.

- One symbolic thing about the naming ceremony is to begin to introduce the child to the values of the society. The norm of truth and honesty is taught the child at this stage of his/her life. This explains why a drop each of water and alcohol is put separately on the baby's tongue with the reminder "if you taste water, say that it is water and if you taste alcohol, say that it is alcohol". In contemporary times, some Christians use water and non-alcoholic beverage to administer this value of truthfulness. Anyhow, this ritual teaches the child to distinguish one thing from another, truth from lie for that matter. It should be noted that lying among the Ghanaian is very much loathed because a liar is as well a murderer.

- It is not uncommon today to see some parents taking their children to the church for naming quite contrary to the age-old tradition.

- A wide range of names are there to choose from, but a name borne by the Ghanaian is not by mere chance, traditionally, names give identity and tell a full story about the bearer. A typical Ghanaian will have at least 3 different names to constitute his full name.

- At official naming, Ghanaians give names based on several factors. Names therefore reflect meanings and tell much about the bearer's identity. The types of name include:

  » Day or Soul name (e. g. Kwame)

  » providential or belief in God (e.g. Onyameba, meaning *God's child*, Nyamekye, meaning *God's gift*)

  » order of birth (e.g. Mansa, i.e. a third successive daughter; Tawiah – one who comes directly after twins),

  » number in which one came in the case of twins, triplets, etc. (e.g. Atsu, Etse, Kakra)

  » circumstance of birth (e.g. Agble i.e. born in the farm; Anto i.e. the father died before he was born)

  » proverbial view of life (e.g. Obidie, Amewuga)

  » named after an ancestor (e.g. Nana)

  » named after a (smaller) deity (e.g. Husunu)

  » origin or family name or surname (e.g. Sraku)

  » Christian name following the introduction of Christianity (e.g. Daniel)

- In modern times, naming ceremonies have added a new dimension of introducing the child to the larger community amidst feasting and merry making later in the day. This new dimension which is known as out-dooring has very much gained ground in many communities.

FORMAL AND INFORMAL EDUCATION (TIT-BITS)

- Close to 80% of children of school-going age are in school (as at 2016). FCUBE (Free Compulsory Universal Basic Education) policy in practice

- Basic level education is 9 years comprising 6 years primary and 3 years Junior High level

- SHS/Technical/Vocational level runs for 3 years after which one can proceed to do tertiary education

- Tuition is free in the government Basic and High Schools. Quality of private Basic schools, however, tend to be better than public schools

- Government interventions to step up the numbers at the basic level includes one free hot meal a day for selected schools, free textbooks for all public basic schools, free uniform for some needy students and scholarships for selected female Science students at the SHS level. In 2017, the government rolled out free SHS for students in public schools

- Ghana has 11 public Universities, 7 Technical Universities, 3 Polytechnics, plus several private Universities owned by religious groups and other organizations and individuals

- One year National Service for all graduates of tertiary Institutions, although military service is not a compulsory component

Informal education

Informal education is acquired from kith and kin and the society at large. Hence the immediate parents, family and clan heads, village and Paramount Chiefs all play a role in informal education by means of reward and punishment, folktales/story-telling, myths and legends, proverbs, folk songs, taboos, norms, ceremonies, traditional art symbols and rites.

Culture

- Titles: Ghanaians are very respectful to the extent that they hardly would address someone older than them or higher in status merely by their names. The norm is to use one's title: Mr./Mrs./Nana, etc.. For adult ladies, the tendency is to address them as *Madam* when not certain about her marital status and/or about her name. To show good sense of bond and respect, elder siblings are addressed by their younger ones as *Brother* (or *Braa* for males) and *Sister* for females. No offence therefore when one calls you *Sister Janet* even though there is no blood relation between you and her; she's only being respectful.

- Handshake, until the advent of Covid-19, used to be one sure way of expressing friendship among Ghanaians.

- Traditionally, every guest or visitor to a house is first offered water even before greetings are exchanged. This is so because water is life, peace and tranquility. This practice was very important as, in the past, people had to trek or walk long distance in order to visit. Hence, water is to quench the thirst. Another reason for offering water to a guest or visitor in the past was to ascertain whether the visitor is indeed a human being and not a ghost.

- Inheritance and succession are mainly along matrilineal lines among the Akan but is through the paternal line among the rest of the people. However, there is the Intestate Succession Law to take care of inheritance challenges in cases where people die intestate.

Rites of passage

- **Puberty rites**

- **Marriage**

- **Death and funerals:** There is a traditional belief in reincarnation. Ancestors are considered as part of the family, although invisible by the living. They are believed to visit their ancestral homes now and then, particularly in the night, and are expected not to be starved when they come. Hence the traditional practice, particularly in the olden days, of leaving the utensils unwashed after the evening meal until the next morning. Water pots were also never left dry; else one was expected to incur the withdrawal – sometimes the wrath – of the ancestors.

- **Religious belief and practice:** The Ghanaian traditionally believes in God as the creator of the universe. He is one with unparalleled attributes as is reflected in the names and several appellations by which He is known. Examples include *Onyankupon* by the Akan and *Mawu Sogbolisa* by the Ewe. God is seen as the all-powerful being at the apex and has divulged

His powers to lesser gods and spirits to enhance our relationship with Him. This arrangement saves Him from unnecessary bother by us. The hierarchy of gods is best explained in the diagram below.

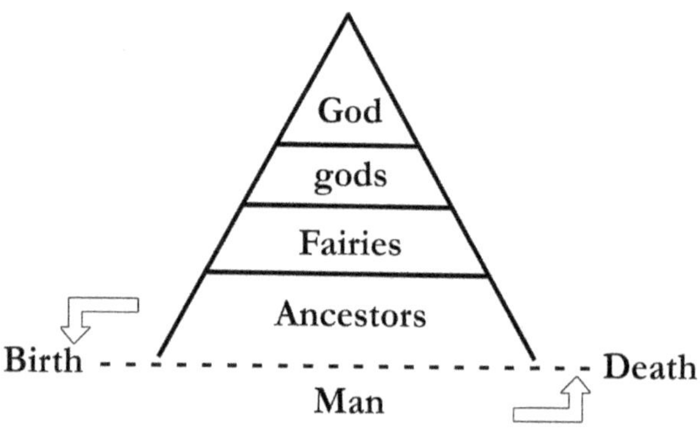

- The ancestors at the lower point of the echelon are the closest to us – the living – and hence take care of our basic immediate needs such as good health and success. The living can commune with them through libation prayer and sacrifice. By virtue of their position, the ancestors can cross the transition line and be born as re-incarnated. The living can also cross the transition line through death and join the realm of ancestors. To qualify as an ancestor however, one must have led a good and virtuous life and must not die too young.

Traditional Festivals

There are several seasonal traditional festivals mostly to commemorate the migration of one community or another into present Ghana, or socio-economic festival marking the beginning or close of agricultural season. Others are to honor ancestors through sacrifice and to forge spiritual affinity. Examples include Aboakyir in Winneba in May, Bakatue in Elmina in July, and Homowo in Accra in August.

Chieftaincy Institution

Chieftaincy is a hierarchical institution among communities and ethnic groups. Chieftaincy runs alongside the national government. Chiefs are custodians of the land and of their respective customs. The Chief has responsibility for the security, well-being and progress of their subjects. Today, we find that most of them have instituted Education Endowment Funds for their communities. The **Asantehene** (King of Asante) is a classic example of modern royalty. Public events by the royalty are always showcases of all aesthetic and spiritual aspects of the Ghanaian culture, namely regalia and paraphernalia, music and dance, palace courtesies, hierarchy, etc.

Akan Clans and Totems

- Totems are widespread among the Akan

- A totem is usually an animal set apart by a clan or community or class of people (e.g. twins) to rely on for spiritual inspiration and/or protection

- The relationship is founded on the symbolic qualities of the animal, which quality the chiefs and clan members must adopt

- Totemic practices presume a belief in some kind of close relationship between the members of the group and the creatures, e. g. snail, bird.

Land issues

Land in Ghana is classified under 4 main types in terms of ownership:

- Stool land

- Family land

- Individual land

- State land, which currently (2016) constitutes 20% of Ghana's land,

NB: Stool land can only legitimately be sold by a properly gazetted Chief who is recognized by the Regional House of Chiefs.

BORBORBOR ENSEMBLE

- Music and dance constitute an important aspect of the Ghanaian. This is manifested in many aspects of their life, i,e. work, social encounters and mourning

- Borborbor is probably the most popular ensembles (dance) in the Volta Region and is undoubtedly widespread across the country

- The name Borborbor stems from the bending posture of the dancers

- Borborbor started in the 1950s, just before Ghana's Independence

- It was started at Kpando by a native Police officer, then called Kwadzo Nuatror, who originally named the group Kpando Borborbor Band

- The Band was however later adopted by Kwame Nkrumah (in the thick of the struggle for Independence) and was renamed Kwame Nkrumah Borborbor Band. It is said that the first time Nkrumah witnessed the group perform at Kpando Residency, he could not help but jump into the ring and start dancing

- This mixed band comprising mainly the youth supported CPP in its political campaigns in the 1950s, which led to the opposition parties boycotting Borborbor but rather embracing Tuidzi and Akpesse ensembles

- Borborbor was proscribed following the 1966 coup and Kwadzo Nuatror was even imprisoned in Ussher Fort whilst the musical instruments of the band were seized and sent to the Castle, then the seat of Government.

The ban was however lifted just before the 2nd Republic and Kwadzo Nuatror was released and engaged by the same military government

- Borborbor has remained a social dance performed at any function at all, including worship by some Orthodox churches particularly Catholic and Evangelical Presbyterian (E.P.) Church

- Borborbor is traditionally performed with 5 basic drums (some of the best quality drums can be bought around Peki that boast several good carvers)

- Borborbor has no basic movement, but the dancers usually use two white handkerchiefs which they keep rolling, whilst bending and shaking their waist. The handkerchiefs were to prevent the hands from doing anything profane and indecent when dancing unlike Tuidzi and Akpesse (refer to "tuidzi mana ga wo")

- Modern form of Borborbor allows the trumpet to be used at certain intervals to allow the singers to rest and also dance

- According to Dr. Agor (a musicologist), Borborbor which is mainly dominant in central and northern Volta, has 7-tone scale (hecta-tonic) while Agbadza (dominant in southern Volta) has 5-tone scale. However, southern dances easily accept the 7-tone scale. Hence, Agbadza can be danced when Borborbor is playing and vice-versa.

Appendix: Day Names among the Akan and Ewe of Ghana

Day	Male (Akan/Guan)	Female (Akan/Guan)	Male (Ewe)	Female (Ewe)
Monday	Kwadwo, Kojo	Adwoa	Kodzo, Kudzo	Adzo,
Tuesday	Kwabena	Abena	Komla/Korbla	Abla, Abra
Wednesday	Kweku, Kwaku	Akua, Ekua	Korku, Koku	Aku
Thursday	Yaw	Yaa	Yao	Yawa
Friday	Kofi	Afia, Afua, Efua	Kofi	Afi
Saturday	Kwame	Ama	Kwami	Ami, Ama
Sunday	Kwasi, Kwesi	Esi, Akosua	Korsi	Esi

ABOUT THE AUTHORS

Cosmos Ata Sracooh is widely recognised as one of Ghana's leading authority in the field of tourism and hospitality. He is a master tour guide, educator, and mentor to many. A graduate of the University of Ghana, he has spent over two decades at the Hotel, Catering and Tourism Training Institute (HOTCATT) where he developed the signature tour guiding course curriculum and taught several courses. His training program has had an invaluable impact on the lives of hundreds of students, many of whom are successful tour guides operating in Ghana today.

In co-writing this book, Tour Guiding: The Ultimate Guide to Theory & Practice with Kwaku Passah Snr, Sracooh draws on his experience and passion for travel, tourism, hospitality and professionalism to leave a legacy, not only for Ghana 's tourism industry, but for West Africa in general.

When he is not teaching tourism or guiding in the field, Sracooh can be found farming, teaching French to students, listening to news about Africa, or writing poetry that reflect today's society. He lives in Accra, Ghana, with his family.

Agoo, Kwaku Passah Snr is the founder and CEO of Exotic Adventures LTD, one of Ghana's leading tour operating companies. Passah introduced and popularized the use of the term, Agoo, as a way to draw the attention of tourists back to the tour guide during a tour.

Passah's expertise in the tourism industry spans over thirty years. A graduate of the University of Ghana, he began his career as a tour guide and was a recipient of the prestigious National Tour Guide of the Year Award.

He is a part-time instructor at the Hotel, Catering, and Tourism Training Institute (HOTCATT). Passah is a member of the Tour Guides Association of Ghana (TORGAG), serving as its President. He is also a long time member of the Tour Operators Union of Ghana (TOUGHA). In addition, Passah has held several leadership roles including facilitator for Ghana's Ministry of Tourism and Diaspora Relations Training Program for tour guides.

Passah has been invited by several major U.S. universities to visit their campuses to introduce his company's unique travel abroad study programs.

He has written a number of articles for some Ghanaian dailies. Passah enjoys gardening, green places, pristine beaches, local food, music and travelling. He lives with his family at Dodowa in Ghana.

REFERENCES

A History of Ghana, Updated and Revised, F. K. Buah, 1998

Short History of Ghana, W.E. Ward, 1960

A History of West Africa 1000-1800, Basil Davidson et al., 1966

Official Tourist Guide of Ghana, 2013-15

Golden Handbook of Ghana, Agona Media

Forts and Castles of Ghana, Albert van Dantzig, 1980

Dear Nana: Letters to My Ancestor, Archbishop Peter K. Sarpong, 1998

Dear Nana: Letters from My ancestor, Archbishop Peter K. Sarpong

Follow Me, Judi Cross

Elmina, The Castle & The Slave Trade, Ato Eshun, 2004

Romancing Ghanaland: The Beauty of Ten Regions, Kofi Akpabli

Harmattan: A Cultural Profile of Northern Ghana, Kofi Akpabli

The Transatlantic Slave Trade: Landmarks, Legacies, expectations, edited by Kwesi Anquandah, N. Jane Opoku and Michel R. Doortmont, 2007

The Heart of Old Accra: where History and Culture Meet, published by Multicultural Urban Design (Africa) Limited, 2006

Navorongo Cathedral: The merge of two cultures, CRAterre Editions, November 2004

An Outline of Historical Events in Ghana, Part 1: 1471 - 1957, George O. Owusu, published by Paramount Printing Works, 1996

A Sense of Savannah – Tales of a Friendly Walk through Northern Ghana, Kofi Akpabli

Ghana Regional Boundaries and Regional Integration, by Raymon Baglo Bening, 1999

The Migration Saga of the Anlo-Ewes of Ghana, Agbotadua Kumassah, 2004

Stones Tell Stories at Osu, by Nii-Adziri Wellington, 2nd Edition, 2017